SAMUEL L. BRENGLE'S HOLY LIFE SERIES

RESURRECTION LIFE
AND POWER

Bob Hostetler, General Editor

wesleyan
PUBLISHING HOUSE
wphstore.com

CREST BOOKS

Copyright © 2016 by The Salvation Army
Published by Wesleyan Publishing House
Indianapolis, Indiana 46250
Printed in the United States of America
ISBN: 978-1-63257-074-1
ISBN (e-book): 978-1-63257-075-8

Library of Congress Cataloging-in-Publication Data

Brengle, Samuel Logan, 1860-1936.
  Resurrection life and power / Samuel L. Brengle ; Bob Hostetler, general editor.
     pages cm. -- (Samuel L. Brengle's holy life series)
  Originally published: London : Salvationist Pub. and Supplies, 1953.
  ISBN 978-1-63257-074-1 (pbk.)
  1. Resurrection. 2. Christian life. I. Hostetler, Bob, 1958- editor. II. Title.
  BT873.B74 2016
  232'.5--dc23
                              2015035642

Contents

Preface

Samuel Logan Brengle was an influential author, teacher, and preacher on the doctrine of holiness in the late nineteenth to early twentieth century, serving from 1887–1931 as an active officer (minister) in The Salvation Army. In 1889 while he and his wife, Elizabeth Swift Brengle, were serving as corps officers (pastors) in Boston, Massachusetts, a brick thrown by a street "tough" smashed Brengle's head against a door frame and caused an injury severe enough to require more than nineteen months of convalescence. During that treatment and recuperation period, he began writing articles on holiness for The Salvation Army's publication, *The War Cry*, which were later collected and published as a "little red book" under the title *Helps to Holiness*. That book's success led to eight others over the next forty-five years: *Heart Talks on Holiness*, *The Way of Holiness*, *The Soul-Winner's Secret*, *When the Holy Ghost Is Come*, *Love-Slaves*, *Resurrection Life and Power*,

Ancient Prophets and Modern Problems, and *The Guest of the Soul*
(published in his retirement in 1934).

By the time of his death in 1936, Commissioner Brengle was an internationally renowned preacher and worldwide ambassador of holiness.
His influence continues today, perhaps more than any Salvationist in
history besides the founders, William and Catherine Booth.

I hope that the revised and updated editions of his books that
comprise the Samuel L. Brengle's Holy Life Series will enhance and
enlarge that influence, introduce these writings to new readers, and
create fresh interest in those who already know the godly wisdom and
life-changing power of these volumes.

While I have taken care to preserve the integrity, impact, and voice
of the original writing, I have carefully and prayerfully made changes
that I hope will facilitate greater understanding and appreciation of
Brengle's words for modern readers. These changes include:

- Revising archaic terms (such as the use of King James English) and
  updating the language to reflect more contemporary usage (such as
  occasionally employing more inclusive gender references);
- Shortening and simplifying sentence structure and revising
  punctuation to conform more closely to contemporary practice;
- Explaining specific references of The Salvation Army that will
  not be familiar to the general population;
- Updating Scripture references (when possible retaining the King
  James Version—used exclusively in Brengle's writings—but frequently incorporating modern versions, especially when doing
  so will aid the reader's comprehension and enjoyment);

- Replacing Roman numerals with Arabic numerals and spelled out Scripture references for the sake of those who are less familiar with the Bible;
- Citing Scripture quotes not referenced in the original and noting the sources for quotes, lines from hymns, etc.;
- Aligning all quoted material to the source (Brengle, who often quoted not only Scripture, but also poetry from memory, often quoted loosely in speaking and writing);
- Adding occasional explanatory phrases or endnotes to identify people or events that might not be familiar to modern readers;
- Revising or replacing some chapter titles, and (in *Ancient Prophets and Modern Problems*) moving one chapter to later in the book; and
- Deleting the prefaces that introduced each book and epigraphs that preceded some chapters.

In the preface to Brengle's first book, Commissioner (later General) Bramwell Booth wrote, "This book is intended to help every reader of its pages into the immediate enjoyment of Bible holiness. Its writer is an officer of The Salvation Army who, having a gracious experience of the things whereof he writes, has been signally used of God, both in life and testimony, to the sanctifying of the Lord's people, as well as in the salvation of sinners. I commend him and what he has here written down to every lover of God and His kingdom here on earth."

In the preface to Brengle's last book, *The Guest of the Soul*, The Salvation Army's third general (and successor to Bramwell Booth) wrote: "These choice contributions . . . will, I am sure, serve to strengthen the faith of the readers of this book and impress upon them the joyousness of life when the heart has been opened to the Holy Guest of the Soul."

I hope and pray that this updated version of Brengle's writings will further those aims.

—Bob Hostetler

general editor

Resurrection Power 1

With the death of Christ, the hopes of His disciples also died. When the tortured, crucified Jesus gave His last expiring cry on the cross, the disciples' faith suffered a total eclipse. Three years before, with bounding joy and swelling hopes, they had left all to follow Him. They had heard His matchless words. They had seen His wondrous works. They had felt His spirit of infinite compassion and tenderness, of absolute justice, of righteousness, and of holiness, and they were sure that He was their King. They expected at any time to see Him take the reins of the government, assert His authority and power, cast out Pilate and his hated Roman garrison, ascend the throne of David, and restore their fathers' kingdom to greater splendor than that of Solomon's time. So sure were they of this that they wrangled among themselves as to which of them should be the greatest in this ideal kingdom.

Jesus told them plainly that they misunderstood His spirit and mission—that He would be despised, rejected, and killed, but that He would rise again. But they did not understand this. They did not believe it. Peter boldly contradicted Jesus and said this should not be, until Jesus had to rebuke him sharply, saying, "Get away from me, Satan! You are a dangerous trap to me. You are seeing things merely from a human point of view, not from God's" (Matt. 16:23 NLT).

Later they came up to the Passover at Jerusalem and were met by immense throngs of people casting their garments and palm branches before Him, and crying out, "Hosanna to the Son of David! Blessed is he who comes in the name of the Lord! Hosanna in the highest!" (Matt. 21:9 ESV).

How these lowly followers must have exulted in that hour! Now Jesus would ascend the throne. Now He would be a king. Now they would share in His glory, and all of their old neighbors would stare and gape in amazement and envious wonder. But the tide turned. The fickle multitude that had so royally welcomed Him one day were crying out, "Crucify Him," the next, and instead of ascending a throne He was hung upon a cross. He had a crown upon His head, but it was of thorns. A man was on His right hand, and another on His left, but they were crucified thieves. He was coming into His kingdom, but it was by the narrow gate of death and the hard way of the tomb. He had talked of His kingdom and glory, but what did this shameful death mean? How could they understand Him? Well, they did not understand, and when He died, their hopes died, too. However, they assisted at His burial, and then, disappointed and disillusioned, they went their way.

They forgot that He had said that He would rise again. Strange that they would forget such a startling statement. But they did forget, or else they might not have become so hopeless. But the fulfillment of God's promises does not depend on our feeble memory of those promises.

Jesus rose as He had said. He laid down His life, and He took it up again. The grave could not hold the Prince of life. He broke its bars. He scattered its darkness. He conquered its terrors. He robbed it of its victory. "O death, where is your victory? O death, where is your sting?" (1 Cor. 15:55 NLT).

The disheartened disciples saw Him. They looked again into His eyes of infinite comprehension and compassion. They listened again to His voice that stirred all the deeps of memory, called forth all the holiest affections, and aroused all the old awe, wonder, and enthusiasm. "By many infallible proofs" (Acts 1:3 KJV) He made them to know that it was He, the very same Jesus whom they had loved and for whom they had forsaken all—the Christ of God; the patient Teacher; the dear Friend; the faithful Reprover; the bold, uncompromising, unfaltering Leader; the deathless Lover; the crucified and dead but now living Redeemer and Savior; their Daysman; their Kinsman; God's Lamb that takes away the sin of the world. On that fateful Good Friday when Jesus died, the bewildered disciples found all their hopes turned to ashes, but on Easter morning the ashes burst into quenchless flame, for Jesus was risen! And many years afterward, Peter—with overflowing gratitude and joy—wrote, "Blessed be the God and Father of our Lord Jesus Christ! According to his great mercy, he has caused us to be born again to a living hope through the resurrection of Jesus Christ from the dead" (1 Pet. 1:3 ESV).

The resurrection was God's complete attestation and vindication of
Jesus as the Christ of God, His well-beloved Son in whom He was
well pleased. At Jesus' baptism, the Holy Spirit, in the form of a dove,
had descended upon Him, and a voice from heaven had declared,
"This is my beloved Son, with whom I am well pleased" (Matt. 3:17
ESV). But later, even John the Baptist began to doubt and sent messengers to Jesus to ask, "Are you the Messiah we've been expecting,
or should we keep looking for someone else?" (Matt. 11:3 NLT). But
the resurrection was God's complete answer to every question, and it
swept away forever every ground of doubt. As Paul declared (in a
complex but wonderful sentence), the lowly, suffering, crucified Jesus
was "declared to be the Son of God in power according to the Spirit
of holiness by his resurrection from the dead" (Rom. 1:4 ESV).

Jesus Christ was the revelation of God. In Him the Father was
unveiled. The Father's heart of love, pity, sympathetic understanding,
and infinite yearning—more tender and unfailing than that of a mother—
was made known in Jesus. In Him, too, was seen the Father's hatred of
sin, His holiness, His spotless purity, His exact and unswerving justice,
and His detestation of all unrighteousness.

Jesus came into the world to reveal the Father and to do the Father's
will. He also came to save lost humanity, to save us from our sins and
from ourselves—from our bad nature, our corruption, our bent toward
evil, our pride, our lust, and our hearts' deceitfulness. He came to bring
us back to God, into reunion with God, in our affections, sympathies,
will, and nature. He came to make us holy, happy, dutiful, unafraid
children of the Father once more. And the resurrection was the final
stone in the everlasting foundation on which this work was to be built.

We are saved by faith. Faith links us to God. As we trust Him, He can work in us and do for us. But when we doubt, we frustrate His good will toward us and prevent His love from accomplishing all His kindly purposes for us. We must trust Him or He cannot save us. Jesus was constantly endeavoring to establish faith in His disciples' hearts. He wrought His miracles and uttered His wonderful sayings that they might believe, and yet they continued to fall back into doubt. Tired and weary, He fell asleep one evening in their little boat. A storm swept down upon them and, in a panic, they awakened Him and said, "Teacher, don't you care that we're going to drown?" (Mark 4:38 NLT). He arose, stilled the storm, and quietly asked, "Why are you afraid? Do you still have no faith?" (Mark 4:40 NLT). Again and again He had to ask them why they doubted.

Just before His crucifixion Jesus told them plainly that He had come from the Father and that He was going back to the Father. With a glimpse of fleeting insight and in a burst of enthusiasm they exclaimed, "At last you are speaking plainly and not figuratively. Now we understand. . . . From this we believe that you came from God" (John 16:29–30 NLT). But Jesus knew them better than they knew themselves. He knew that the foundation He was building for their faith and hope was not yet complete. He knew how weak and uncertain their faith was, and He quietly replied, "Do you finally believe? But the time is coming — indeed it's here now — when you will be scattered, each one going his own way, leaving me alone. Yet I am not alone because the Father is with me" (John 16:31–32 NLT).

And true, they left Him alone. They fled away, and He died alone. The foundation of their faith was not fully laid by His life, miracles,

and words, but it was made complete by His resurrection from the
dead. Now they could and would and did believe with a

> Faith that will not shrink,
> Though pressed by every foe;
> That will not tremble on the brink
> Of any earthly woe.[1]

Now they had a foundation for faith on which they could build
God's city, and on which they could stand unshaken and exultant,
"when earth's foundations melt away."[2]

All they needed now was the baptism of Jesus, the baptism with
the Holy Spirit and fire, which would purify their hearts and empower
them "with inner strength through his Spirit" (Eph. 3:16 NLT), that
Christ might live in their hearts by faith. This, after patient waiting and
fervent prayer, they received on the day of Pentecost.

Through the faith perfected in them by Jesus' resurrection, they
were led to wait for and receive His baptism with the Holy Spirit, and
Christ was revealed in their hearts.

With the sure knowledge they now had, and with Christ's Spirit in
them, they had faith to face a frowning world and turn it upside down.
They could now go forth and overthrow every empire of evil and top-
ple every throne founded on injustice and upheld by the pomp of mere
earthly pride and power. With them came the almighty Holy Spirit. All
power in heaven and earth belonged to their Master, and they were His
ministers, His ambassadors. He was behind them, with them, and in
them, and His Spirit went before them. They spoke and worked by

His authority, and all His infinite resources of power, love, patience, and long-suffering were at the disposal of their faith. They could ask for what was needed to accomplish the superhuman task He had given them, and it would be given to them. They were insufficient of themselves for their work, but their sufficiency was of God. They were to know the power of His resurrection and be made partakers of that power. The power that had raised their Master from the dead was the same power that worked in them. Oh, the wonder of it! It inspired them. It thrilled them. It made them unafraid and unconquerable in the face of all the massed and mocking forces of sin and hell.

They looked into the eyes of their foes without quailing. They faced whippings, stonings, and imprisonments without faltering. If they suffered for the cause and name of their dear Master, they counted it a joy. When they were imprisoned, they sang psalms in the night, and the jailer became a Christian. They rejoiced in tribulation. They gloried in affliction and distress. They smiled at death, for they knew it had no sting for them. They shouted over the grave, for it was already spoiled and robbed of its victory. They posted over land and sea to tell all the world the wondrous story of the resurrection. And everywhere they went, the heavenly power went with them, and hoary superstitions and the haunting fears of sin's dark night began to vanish away.

Henceforth, for them to live was Christ, and to die was gain (see Phil. 1:21). He was the Vine, they were the branches, and as the branch receives life and power from the vine, so their life and power were from Christ. And as the vine produces fruit through the branches, so the fruit of Christ's life and Spirit was formed in them.

In Him was sacrificial, deathless love, and this love was reproduced in them. Oh, how they loved! They loved their enemies. They
prayed for their persecutors. When Stephen was stoned to death, he
prayed, "Lord, don't charge them with this sin!" (Acts 7:60 NLT). And
Paul, when the love of some of his brothers failed, wrote, "I will
gladly spend myself and all I have for you, even though it seems that
the more I love you, the less you love me" (2 Cor. 12:15 NLT).

Joy, the very joy of Jesus, was perfected in them. He bequeathed
His joy to them (see John 15:11). When He died, He was so poor He
had little to leave them but His joy. But what a treasure!

With that joy, He also left them His peace. "Peace I leave with
you" (John 14:27 KJV). It was the resurrection peace, the peace of an
assured and endless life over which death has no power. Storms might
rage around them, but that deep central peace flowed on undisturbed,
for it flowed into them from the Father, through their union with the
resurrected Jesus.

Patience was perfected in them. Eternity was in their hearts. They
were no longer creatures of time, and they could well afford to wait
and bear long with the poor slaves of sin around them, as their dear
Savior did. Oh, how patient He had been with them! And for His sake
and by His indwelling Spirit they, too, became patient.

The gentleness, goodness, faith, and meekness of their Lord were
also reproduced in them and made manifest in word and deed. It was
Christ living His life in them.

Can this resurrection life and power be yours and mine? Yes, it is
for all. It is for every living branch, great or small, that is in the true
Vine. Do you believe that He rose from the dead? Do you believe that

He is the living Christ and not simply a dead Jew in a Jerusalem grave? And do you with joy confess this with your mouth? Then this resurrection life and power and undying hope is yours, if you will receive it. "If you openly declare that Jesus is Lord and believe in your heart that God raised him from the dead, you will be saved" (Rom. 10:9 NLT), and in that salvation are all the vast powers and deathless hopes and overflowing joys of His resurrection life, to be drawn upon by faith, as those with an account draw money from their bank to meet their need. And now according to our faith it will be unto us.

> No human or angelic mind
> Had ever dreamed the Son of God
> On Calvary's cruel cross should die
> To save us by His precious blood.
> He died for rebels; now He lives
> And reigns for us in glory bright;
> His precious blood in peace He pleads
> For us, the newborn sons of light.[3]

All is ours, since we are Christ's and Christ is God's.

NOTES

1. William Hiley Bathurst, "Oh, for a Faith That Will Not Shrink," 1831, public domain.

2. Johann A. Rothe, "Now I Have Found the Ground Wherein," trans. John Wesley, 1754, public domain.

3. Author unknown, "When Christ the Lord at God's Command," *Salvation Army Songs,* comp. William Booth (London: The Salvation Army Book Department, 1911), 568.

Evidences and Practical Lessons 2

After John the Baptist died, his amazed and sorrowful disciples buried him then went and told Jesus, and from that time we hear no more of them. They ceased to be a distinct company of men. The power that united them failed in John's death, and they fell apart and were soon lost in the crowd.

When Jesus died and was buried, we find the same disintegrating forces at work among His disciples. Amazed, disappointed, and heartbroken, they said, "We had hoped that he was the one to redeem Israel" (Luke 24:21 ESV), and they started for their homes.

But a wonderful thing happened. Jesus' scattering, discomfited disciples were rallied by the strange story that His grave was empty, that an angel had been seen sitting in the vacant tomb, that a vision of angels had said He was alive, and that Jesus Himself had appeared to certain of their company. From that hour we find the power that bound them together strengthening until some fifty days later, on the day of Pentecost, by the descent of the Holy Spirit upon them, they are welded into a divine oneness such as was never known before, and Jesus' prayer—that they might be one, even as He and the Father are one—was answered.

How different are the graves of John and Jesus! That of John is still shrouded in darkness, but that of Jesus is aflame with light. It is the first rift in the surrounding gloom through which we look up into the face of angels, see the future world, and get foregleams of the full glory yet to be revealed.

In the presence of Jesus' resurrection, all other miracles pale like the stars before the rising sun. It is the crowning evidence that He is the Son of God, and that "as the Father has life in Himself, so He has granted the Son to have life in Himself" (John 5:26 NKJV), with power to destroy death and give eternal life to those who believe in His name.

> The strife is o'er, the battle done;
> The victory of life is won;
> The song of triumph has begun.[1]

But how do we know that He rose again?

1. We know it by the testimony of those who saw Him: the women, Peter, the two on the road to Emmaus, the other disciples, and then some five hundred to whom He showed Himself. And, finally, Paul, like a baby whose birth was long overdue (see 1 Cor. 15:8).

Again and again, under varying circumstances and before increasing numbers of unimpeachable witnesses, Jesus showed Himself, until the last vestige of doubt that their Lord had risen vanished from the disciples' minds. And this became the foundational fact upon which they took their stand and preached that He was the Son of God—preached with such power that their very enemies were won over by the thousands and a great company of the priests who had consented to and demanded Jesus' death were obedient to the faith (see Acts 6:7). They testified to it, preached it, wrote about it, gloried in it, triumphed over all their fears, and faced martyrdom, joyously dying in that faith.

2. We know it by the fact that the disciples—though they were poor and unlearned, despised and hated, and at first were bewildered and confounded by their Master's death—were not scattered and lost as John's disciples were, but were joined together in a far stronger and more vital and joyous union after the death of Jesus than when He was with them in the flesh.

3. We know it by the church that dates back to within fifty days of the death of Jesus, and was built upon the faith that He arose from the dead. Such an institution as the Christian church could not have been built upon a falsehood.

4. But the most vital evidence of Jesus' resurrection—that which brings the most complete satisfaction to the heart that comes into possession of it and confirms all other evidence—is that which is given to us individually with the baptism of the Holy Spirit.

When my friend in New York sails for Liverpool, how do I know that he has arrived safely? I know it by the cablegram or letter he sends back to me. How do I know that Jesus is not dead, but living, not buried still in Joseph's rocky tomb, but risen and ascended to the right hand of the Father where all power in heaven and earth is His?

I know it by the Holy Spirit whom He has sent to me, that fills my whole soul with light and love, and makes me know my risen Lord better than I knew my mother. This is the crowning evidence, which He gives to those who obey Him.

The other evidences are historical and general and are to be sifted, considered, and weighed as is the evidence of any other historical fact. The evidence given in the baptism of the Holy Spirit is personal and living, confirming the faith of him or her who receives it. The former may satisfy the head; this satisfies the heart.

The external historical evidences are for the natural being. The inward spiritual evidence is for the spiritual being. The first are given once and for all, are never repeated, and cannot be added to nor subtracted from. The latter is repeated as often as God can find a hungry, obedient heart that will be satisfied with nothing short of knowing Jesus and being filled with His Spirit. It is God's new, ever-recurring, ever-living and eternal answer to the soul that from the heart sings, "Thee to know is all my cry."[2]

He has given this evidence to me. Some precious lessons lie on the surface of the Scriptures, but others must be dug for as for silver and gold. Some are learned in the school of obedience and others in the school of affliction. Some are revealed to us by a great burst of light like the sun shining through rifts in thick clouds, and some dawn upon us and unfold so gradually that we can hardly tell when we came into possession of them. So it is with the lessons we learn from Jesus' resurrection.

The first and plainest lesson we learn is that of immortality. In the presence of the risen Jesus, we can confidently say death does not end all. There is life beyond the grave. The tomb, for those who love Him, is merely the narrow portal out of the prison-house of the body into the liberty and light and love of the Father's home.

✗ Our loved ones die, but we do not mourn like those who have no hope. They have outstripped us in the race. They have reached home ahead of us and are watching and waiting for us. Their trials are past. Their warfare is accomplished. All tears are wiped from their eyes. ✗ They are absent from the body but are present with the Lord (see 2 Cor. 5:8). They are with Jesus, and they see His face (see Rev. 12:4). By and by, in a very little while, if we are faithful unto death, we shall meet them again and shall know each other there and be forever with the Lord (see 1 Thess. 4:17).

But there is a deeper lesson than this for us to learn—one that is nearer home and more needful to us in this present life. The apostles labored constantly to make people see and know that the soul, while yet in the body, may enter into the resurrection power of Jesus and rise and walk with Him in newness of life (see Rom. 6:4).

As Jesus after His resurrection was freed from the limitations of the fleshly body, so in Him we can now be free from the limitations of the fleshly spirit—the carnal mind. We can die to sin and be altogether spiritual and holy, and we can live the life of heaven here upon earth, filled with a constant sense of God's favor, having power always to overcome sin and to do the will of God on earth as it is done in heaven.

Paul said we are reconciled to God by Jesus' death, but we are saved by His life (see Rom. 5:10). As we see Him dying for us, our enmity is conquered by His love. We surrender ourselves to Him, and we feel and know that He freely pardons the past. But as we try to live for Him, we find that we are weak and carnal, and again and again we fail until we see that only His life, His Spirit in us, can save and keep us. Then, opening our hearts to Him that He may live in us, we find ourselves saved by His life, cleansed from sin, sanctified wholly, and kept by His power.

As Mary's ointment filled the whole house with perfume after the alabaster box was broken, so the resurrection life and power of the crucified Jesus waits to fill all hearts that will receive Him.

> Lo, a new creation dawning!
> Lo, I rise to life divine!
> In my soul an Easter morning;
> I am Christ's and Christ is mine.[3]

A brilliant young minister came to one of my holiness meetings and wanted to talk with me. When I saw him, he opened his heart and told me what an awful struggle he was having with fleshly temptations, so much so that he would walk the streets almost in agony. He had been reconciled to God by the death of Jesus, but he had not yet learned that he could be saved to the uttermost by His life. But after having the way of holiness explained to him, he yielded himself to Jesus and received Him by faith into his heart. He found himself filled with resurrection power and saved to the uttermost.

Some weeks later he wrote me: "I have burned the last bridge behind me, and am all under the blood. Oh, what weeks these have been since I saw you, such as I never believed could be realized this side of heaven."

Then he continued to relate how his wife got the blessing. A revival broke out in his church, and nearly all the leading members got sanctified, while many wandering souls entered God's kingdom. The fire continued to burn in his heart, the life of Jesus still saved him, and a year later he wrote me that he had had a second revival in his church, with scores of people flocking to the Lord for salvation, while his own soul was "dwelling in Beulah land."[4]

Many years have now passed since I first met him, but the fire still burns in his heart. For years he has been president of a university, where he leads hundreds of young men and women into the fullness of blessing, and teaches and trains them for wise and valiant service. And everywhere and always he testifies how he, a young, struggling, ambitious preacher, found Christ in all fullness at a Salvation Army penitent form (the place where people kneel in the church to pray) with an old drunken "bum" kneeling on one side and a woman of the streets on the other. The glory and power of God accompany his testimony and his ministry.

He received the very same life and Spirit that the disciples had received in the upper room on the day of Pentecost, and it is for you, too. Jesus is not dead, but living. Is He living in your heart? Are you a partaker of His resurrection power? Do you, in Him, have victory over all sin and all devils?

> What profits it that He is risen,
> If dead in sins thou yet dost lie?
> If yet thou cleavest to thy prison,
> What profit that He dwells on high?

What profit that He loosed and broke

All bonds, if ye in league remain

With earth? Who weareth Satan's yoke

Shall call Him Master but in vain.[5]

His life and power is your portion. Rise up in glad faith before Him and claim it now.

NOTES

1. Anonymous hymn, possibly from the twelfth century; translated into English by Francis Pott.

2. Elizabeth MacKenzie, "From My Soul Break Every Fetter," 1887, public domain.

3. Attributed to Francis Bottome, "Precious Jesus, O to Love Thee," 1873, public domain.

4. Charles A. Miles, "Dwelling in Beulah Land," 1911, public domain.

5. Attributed to J. G. Wolff, "Who Follows Christ Whate'er Betide," trans. Catherine Winkworth, 1855, public domain.

Is Death a Mystery? 3

A man who had been blind from his birth said he thought the sun must look like the sound of a bass drum. We smile wisely at this, forgetting that we probably miss the mark quite as far in matters more important, because we approach them with the wrong faculty.

The beauties of a landscape and the glories of the vaulted heavens are not made known to us through the sense of hearing. The harmony of a song is not made known to us by the sense of sight. If we would know the flavor of some fruit, we must not seek to discover it by the sense of touch or sight or smell, but by taste.

We cannot dispose of a question of conscience by an exercise of memory or solve a problem in mathematics by the conscience. Everything we can know is revealed to us through some corresponding sense or faculty, and every other sense and faculty must stand back in utter helplessness while this revelation is made.

Is death a mystery? To every faculty and sense but one it is an awful and unfathomable mystery. We look into the coffin where our precious dead lies and peer into the yawning grave with our poor little reason and understanding, and it is like looking out of our lighted rooms into the impenetrable blackness of a dark and stormy night. It is all heartbreaking amazement, desolation, and mystery. Our understanding is helpless and dumb in the presence of a problem it was not made to solve, and our stricken hearts break under a burden of sorrow that reason cannot lift.

But are we left without any sense or faculty that can lift this burden, soothe this sorrow, or solve this mystery? No, thank God, no! Faith is the faculty with which we must approach this problem, and to faith there is no mystery in death.

To our sainted dead, the coffin is not a narrow and locked prison, but an easy couch of sleep. The grave is not a bottomless abyss, but an open door through which the dear one has passed into the presence of the King, into the unveiled vision of Jesus and the unbroken joys and fellowships of the saints made perfect—a door of escape from the limitations, tears, toils, temptations, and tortures of time into the ageless blessedness of eternity where "God shall wipe away all tears from their eyes; and there shall be no more death, neither sorrow, nor crying, neither shall there be any more pain" (Rev. 21:4 KJV). To faith death simply means that the appointed task in this world's harvest field is done and the dear one has gone home. The day's lessons have been learned, and the Father has come to take His child home from school. Or, some evil was coming from which God in His wisdom saw fit to snatch His loved one (see Isa. 57:1–2).

Faith accepts death as God's appointment. This is a fact to be believed, not to be reasoned over. And if we simply believe it, the sting of death is drawn. But may we not ask why? May we not seek to understand? Yes, but we must do it with great caution, as a blind man feels his way along crowded streets and unknown thoroughfares. And we must do it under the constant leadership of faith, if we do not wish every step to be one of peril and possibly of ruin.

Philosophy may enable us to endure the agony following the death of our loved ones, but only faith nourished and made strong by constant feeding upon the promises and examples of God's Word can enable us to triumph in that hour.

A woman, recently bereft of her mother who was all that she had left of her family and dear ones, wrote that she read and reread the fifteenth chapter of 1 Corinthians, and to that word of God she anchored her faith. And through that word, God comforted her with great comfort. The pain may pierce like a sword and ache like a carbuncle. The sorrow may be inexpressibly bitter and the desolation unutterable, but faith finds its firm footing on God's Word. It grasps the promises and fixes its eyes upon His unchangeable character of wisdom and love, and emerges from the flood and storm chastened, but strengthened—still sorrowing, but triumphant and serene. And we shall be wise if, while still surrounded by our loved ones, we fill our minds and hearts with those precious truths God has revealed, so that when the storm overtakes us, as it someday surely will, we shall be prepared.

Comforted  4

In one of my meetings some time ago, I saw a sight to make all heaven rejoice. Two strong men stood embracing each other and, with faces aglow, sang with all their might, "Hallelujah! 'Tis done! I believe on the Son,"[1] while the others who were there praised the Lord with great joy.

I had seen the marvelous illumination of the Pan-American Exposition and World's Fair, but the illumination on the faces of those two men put that to shame. A light never seen on sea or land, the solar light of heaven, lit up their eyes and beamed from their countenances, and they looked to be carefree—two of the gladdest men in the world. Their joy was clean and pure, unutterable and without alloy.

Who were they? Were they carefree in the blush and glory of life's morning, untouched as yet by its sorrow and unsmitten in its strife and conflict, with all its full pleasures, triumphs, and prizes before them? Were they yet to prove the sweet, pure joys of wedded life and home, and listen for the first time to the prattle of their children and the music of her voice who was to be all their own, who was to be their very other self?

Some months ago one of those men left his home early in the morning and, returning within a few hours, found it—with his wife and children—burned to ashes. He had drunk sorrow's bitterest cup to the dregs and had been swept by desolation's fiercest storms. The other was a precious soul who had stepped onto the ship at Liverpool a few weeks before to return to his darling wife and seven young children, only to be met on landing by the awful word that she was dead and they were motherless.

They were not young men anymore, nor were they old. They were too old to begin life over again with the bounding enthusiasm and confident hopes of youth, and too young to lie down and die. Life's morning was past, and the fierce heat of a noonday sun had smitten them.

What, then, was the secret of their joy? Where was the hiding place of their triumph? The one, to drown his sorrows, had plunged into dissipation and sought to soothe his heartache with drink, only to find that he had forsaken the fountain of living waters and hewed out for himself cisterns—broken cisterns—that could hold no water (see Jer. 2:13). But that night he had returned to the Savior. After a struggle, he had found Jesus, found "peace in believing" (Rom. 15:13 KJV) and "joy in the Holy Spirit" (Rom. 14:17 NLT). And there he and his friend stood embracing each other, rejoicing, comforted, with their broken hearts healed by the touch of the pierced hands, triumphant over all the crushing sorrows of earth and all the malice and rage of hell.

Oh, that men and women would bring their crushed and aching hearts to Jesus, for in Him they would find peace and healing and heart's ease.

I have seen His face in blessing
When my eyes were dimmed with tears;
I have felt His hand caressing
When my heart was torn by fears.
When the shadows gathered o'er me,
And the gloom fell deep as night,
In the darkness, just before me,
There were tokens of His light.

I have stepped in waves of sorrow
Till my soul was covered o'er;
I have dreaded oft the morrow
And the path which lay before.
But when sinking in my sadness,
I have felt His helping hand,
And ere day dawn came to His gladness
With the courage to withstand.

I was wandering, and He found me,
Brought me from the verge of hell;
I was bruised, and He bound me,
Sick was I, He made me well.
I was wounded, and He healed me

When a-wearied of the strife;

I was erring, and He sealed me,

Dead, His Spirit gave me life.

By His life's blood He has claimed me

As a jewel in His sight;

As His own child He has named me,

Brought me forth to walk in light.

So I'm fighting till He calls me,

Walking in the path He trod;

And I care not what befalls me

Living in the life of God.[2]

Are you storm-tossed and troubled and heartbroken? If so, look to the Lord Jesus. He is the great Consoler. He is the Healer of broken hearts. He has the balm for every wound. Has it not been said of His people, "In all their affliction he was afflicted" (Isa. 63:9 KJV)? Does not the mother suffer in her child's suffering? So likewise does He in "our light affliction, which is but for a moment" work out for us "a far more exceeding and eternal weight of glory; while we look not at the things which are seen, but at the things which are not seen: for the things which are seen"—these sufferings and sorrows—"are temporal; but the things which are not seen"—the truths and consolations of the Lord—"are eternal" (2 Cor. 4:17–18 KJV).

We also read, "If we suffer, we shall also reign with him" (2 Tim. 2:12 KJV) and "we suffer with him, that we may be also glorified together" (Rom. 8:17 KJV). The victory of those two men with which this chapter opened was but a foretaste of the blessed time to which all God's children are hastening, when He "shall wipe away all tears from their eyes; and there shall be no more death, neither sorrow, nor crying, neither shall there be any more pain: for the former things are passed away" (Rev. 21:4 KJV).

Come, ye disconsolate, where'er ye languish,
Come to the mercy seat, fervently kneel;
Here bring your wounded hearts, here tell your anguish;
Earth has no sorrow that heaven cannot heal.

Here dwells the Father; love's waters are streaming,
Forth from the throne of God, plenteous and pure;
Come to His temple for mercy redeeming;
Earth has no sorrow that He cannot cure.

Here waits the Savior, gentle and loving,
Ready to meet us, His grace to reveal;
On Him cast the burden, trustfully coming;
Earth has no sorrow that heaven cannot heal.

Here speaks the Comforter, Light of the straying,
Hope of the penitent, Advocate sure,
Joy of the desolate, tenderly saying,
"Earth has no sorrow My grace cannot cure."[3]

NOTES

1. Philip P. Bliss, "Hallelujah! 'Tis Done," 1874, public domain.

2. William John McAlnan, "I Have Seen His Face in Blessing," 1894, public domain.

3. Thomas Moore, "Come, Ye Disconsolate," 1816, public domain.

Meditations on the Resurrection 5

SUNDAY

The great preacher John Jasper, of Richmond, Virginia, during a funeral sermon looked down as though peering into the yawning grave of the whole earth and cried out, "Grave! Grave! Oh Grave! Where is your victory? I hear you've got a mighty banner down there and terrorize everyone who comes along this way. Bring out your armies and furl your banners of victory. Show me your hand and let them see what you can do." Then he made the dramatic reply, in the voice of the grave, "Ain't got no victory now; *had* victory, but King Jesus passed through this country and tore my banners down. He says His people shan't be troubled any more forever; and He tells me to open the gates and let them pass on their way to glory."

A young man who had just lost his young wife after ten months of married bliss wrote me the other day: "Oh, hallelujah! My heart aches, but it also leaps with joy to think that my Louise is in heaven with Jesus!"

That is the message of Easter. The grave has no victory (see 1 Cor. 15:55). It does not hold our treasures. To be absent from the body is to be present with the Lord, and to those who love the Lord, death is merely the narrow gateway into that life without tears or pain or fear of parting.

MONDAY

Hope looks upward and onward with glad expectancy and is unknown except among Christians. The godless world is hopeless. Hundreds of millions in China look back and down, worshiping their ancestors. Hundreds of millions of Hindus long to be lost in vague unconsciousness because active life to them is full of terrors. But since Jesus was resurrected, the Christian is jubilant with hope. The grave has no terrors for us, for we know we will never lie down in it—it only receives our cast-off bodies. We will live because our Lord lives. We will never die, but will someday simply move out of the tenement of our perishing bodies and be forever with the Lord. Our friends who died in the Lord are not dead, but living, robed in splendor, throned in light, washed from every stain, and freed from every throb of pain. Blessed be God for the streams of light pouring forth from the open and empty grave of Jesus, flooding the future with joyous hope—hope that lights up the face with radiance and "does not put us to shame" (Rom. 5:5 ESV).

Be strong, my soul!

Thy loved ones go

Within the veil. God's thine, e'en so.

Be strong!

Be strong, my soul!

Death looms in view.

Lo, here thy God! He'll bear thee through.

Be strong![1]

TUESDAY

The sorrowful women had returned from Jesus' grave with an unbelievable story. It was empty, and two men in shining garments had told them He was not there, but was risen. The women told the dazed disciples, but to them it was an idle tale. Their hearts were still numb from the scenes of the crucifixion and the awful shock of His death, and they could not believe. But soon the glorious fact of His resurrection burst upon them—was forced upon them—and they immediately set all Jerusalem in an uproar, began to turn the world upside down (see Acts 17:6), and the world began to roll "out of the darkness into his wonderful light" (1 Pet. 2:9 NLT).

But there are still those to whom this glad story is just an idle tale. I knew a mother who lived near a church where this fact was constantly witnessed to, but to her it was an idle tale, and for years—with a face of unutterable sadness—she went weekly to her little boy's grave, refusing to be comforted. She might as well have lived before the resurrection, for it gave her no comfort. She believed not.

Is it so with you? Do not refuse to be comforted. He is risen, and our dead who die in the Lord are not in the grave, but with Him in paradise.

WEDNESDAY

"I am not ashamed of the gospel of Christ," wrote Paul (Rom. 1:16 KJV). And well might he so write, for it is the very fullness and perfection of good news, not only in word but in act, not only in promise but in fulfillment, not alone in prophecy but in realization.

The words and performance of Jesus match each other exactly and make the completed gospel. He never spoke of death as we do. He called it sleep: "The girl isn't dead; she's only asleep" (Matt. 9:24 NLT) and, "Our friend Lazarus has fallen asleep" (John 11:11 NLT). And by His word He awakened them from the sleep that we call death.

"I am the . . . life," He declared. "Everyone who lives in me and believes in me will never ever die" (John 11:25–26 NLT). And when they thought He was dead, and sought Him in the grave among the dead, He suddenly appeared before them in imperishable life. This is the completed gospel which, believed, is the power of God unto salvation.

It thrilled the dying ancient world with new life and hope. It pierced the awful darkness and gloom with heavenly light. Slaves heard it, believed, and rose up free men and women in Christ Jesus. Bigoted Pharisees and proud philosophers heard it and became humble followers of Jesus. The vilest drunkards, prostitutes, thieves, and murderers heard it with joy and became saints. It was the power of God unto their salvation, and it has lost none of its power.

THURSDAY

"He is not here," declared the two angels to the sorrowful women who came to the grave on that first Easter morning (Luke 24:6 KJV). And indeed He had not been there except to claim again the bruised and torn body that had been laid there. He had been in paradise with the blessed thief who trusted Him and whom He saved on the cross. His body was but His temple. "Destroy this temple, and in three days I will raise it up," He said. "But when Jesus said 'this temple,' he meant his own body" (John 2:19, 21 NLT). We must not confuse the temple with the worshiper within the temple. The temple may decay and fall into ruin, but the worshiper still lives on in other scenes. Our precious dead are not in the dark, damp graves; they are in mansions of light and love, at home with the Lord if they died in Him. It can be said of every one of them as it was of Jesus, "He is not here." It is only their bodily temples that we lay in the grave.

FRIDAY

"Can the dead live again?" asked Job (Job 14:14 NLT). But what of those who never die? "Everyone who lives in me and believes in me will never ever die," said Jesus to sorrowing Martha (John 11:26 NLT).

That which we call death—the separation of the soul from the body—was never so called by Jesus and Paul. They called it sleep. They reserved the dreaded word *death* for that more awful state—the separation of the soul from God. Eternal life is more than eternal existence; it is eternal blessedness in union with God.

And that wonderful experience can begin here and now for all who with penitent faith lay hold on Christ, and what we call death cannot destroy that blessedness. It only frees it from earthly limitations. The bird in the cage lives in the atmosphere. When the cage is opened and the bird flies forth, it still lives in the atmosphere, but without limitations. Our body is our cage. We live and move and have our being in God while in the body, but when we escape from it and leave it empty, we still live in God. To trust and love and obey God is to live in Him. Not to believe in Him—to disobey Him and be out of sympathy with Him—that is to die, indeed, and to be fixed in that state forever is eternal death.

O my soul, when you love and trust and obey, you have the life that is everlasting. Death cannot touch you. And when people say, "He is dead," you shall be reveling in fullness of life.

SATURDAY

Yesterday I read a fine article and exhortation by a brother who urges us to get ready because eternity is coming. Eternity is not coming. Eternity is here. We are enwrapped by it. It arches over us as do the heavens above us. It enfolds us as does the atmosphere about us. We call that little period in which we live in our bodies "time," and when we lay off the body, we say we shall enter into "eternity." It is as though the deep-sea diver should say, "If I should now get out of my diving suit, I should be in the ocean." He is in the ocean now, only its power to effect him is limited by the suit. If he got out of his suit, the ocean would swallow him up. So eternity will swallow us up and work our everlasting undoing unless we learn to live the eternal life while in the body. John Wesley said that the one who lives a truly religious life is now living in eternity.

We are now becoming what we shall ever be—lovers of God and the things of God, or haters of God and the things of God. We are now learning the sweet and heavenly art of loving, trusting, and obeying God, fitting ourselves to live in eternity. Or else by unbelief, disobedience, and selfishness, we are forming ourselves into vessels of wrath and dishonor, and hastening to endless darkness, loneliness, and woe. Where will you spend the rest of eternity?

NOTE

1. Anonymous, *The Lutheran Witness* 18, no. 4 (July 21, 1899): 1.

What Is Fundamental? 6

Recently two leading Christian denominations met in annual assembly, and these conventions flamed with doctrinal discussion and dissension, while newspapers — always eager for such reports — scattered (and are still scattering) the fire. There has probably been no period of greater doctrinal unrest since the days of Luther and Calvin and Knox than at the present time. No article of faith is too sacred to be questioned, no doctrine is too precious to be hurled into the seven-times-heated furnace of debate and tried in the hot fires of public discussion.

But no devoted, believing heart need faint. It is not the first time that a trial of truth has been made by such fire. The Son of God knows all about the furnace, and He keeps watch over His own. He still walks in the midst of the fire as He did in old Babylon (see Dan. 3), protecting that which is true, so that there shall not be even the smell of fire upon it. And it is ever so that "truth, crushed to earth, shall rise again."[1]

If there is any chaff mixed with the wheat of sound doctrine, it is well that the winnowing should blow it away. But the wheat must be saved, or men and women will grope in spiritual uncertainty and perish of soul-hunger.

The truth can be known and not simply guessed at. Jesus said to some who had believed in Him, "You are truly my disciples if you remain faithful to my teachings. *And you will know the truth*" (John 8:31–32 NLT, emphasis added).

Some doctrines can be verified in soul-satisfying experiences. When we, brokenhearted on account of our sin, look to Jesus, seeking forgiveness, and the burden rolls away, we know it. When we pass from the death of sin into the life of holiness, we know it. When the Holy Spirit reveals Christ within us, we know it. When the Bible suddenly flames with light, revealing all the hidden things of our secret life, the deep needs of our soul, and all God's ample provisions of grace, we know it. When Jesus (whom we despised) suddenly becomes to us altogether lovely, and the will of God (which was to us a galling yoke) now becomes our delight, we know it.

"We *know* that we have passed from death unto life" (1 John 3:14 KJV, emphasis added). "Anyone who loves is a child of God and *knows* God" (1 John 4:7 NLT, emphasis added). "By this we *know* that we abide in him and he in us, because he has given us of his Spirit" (1 John 4:13 ESV, emphasis added). "We *know* that God's children do not make a practice of sinning. . . . We *know* that we are children of God and that the world around us is under the control of the evil one. And we *know* that the Son of God has come, and he has given us understanding so that we can *know* the true God. And now we live in fellowship with the true God because we live in fellowship with his Son, Jesus Christ" (1 John 5:18–20 NLT, emphasis added). "When I am raised to life again, you will *know* that I am in my Father, and you are in me, and I am in you" (John 14:20 NLT, emphasis added). "And we have received God's Spirit (not the world's spirit), so we can *know* the wonderful things God has freely given us" (1 Cor. 2:12 NLT, emphasis added).

Thank God there are some certainties that are not settled by debate but by tasting and seeing that the Lord is good (see Ps. 34:8).

Some newspapers are full of the wordy attacks and counterattacks of so-called "fundamentalists" and "modernists." But I reckon that those great doctrines that can be verified in conscious experience are the fundamentals of the Christian faith. We must begin with those. We must be born again to see the kingdom of God and the things of the kingdom. Some things are learned not by debate and much study but by doing: "Anyone who wants to do the will of God will know whether my teaching is from God or is merely my own" (John 7:17 NLT).

One day something marvelous and transforming happened to Paul. He said, "It pleased God . . . to reveal his Son in me" (Gal. 1:15–16 KJV). And Paul did not consider this experience something peculiar to himself, for he wrote to his Corinthian brothers and sisters, and said, "Surely you know that Jesus Christ is among you; if not, you have failed the test of genuine faith" (2 Cor. 13:5 NLT).

Paul and Luke were dear and intimate friends, but I do not think, after the wonder of this spiritual revelation of Christ in him, Paul ever spent any time splitting hairs and arguing with Luke about the biological reasonableness of his story of the virgin birth of Jesus, so far did the spiritual wonder of his experience of Christ formed within him excel the natural wonder of the virgin's experience.

Some time ago a venerable archdeacon of the Episcopal church, sixty years of age, came to see me about his soul. He was brought up a Wesleyan, and he knew a great number of Wesley's hymns by heart. For years he had preached in the Methodist church before uniting with the Episcopal church. He is probably as well versed in theology as I, or better. He believes the truths I believe and is grounded in sound doctrine, but he was restless and uncertain and afraid. He had no peace. But as we prayed, and he looked unto Jesus, peace came to his heart, and some days later I received from him a letter telling of his joy. "Yesterday and today are days of heaven upon earth," he wrote. "I am possessed by a holy stillness, a blessed quietness. I am becalmed in Christ. Praise God!"

He wrote further, "I seem to grow by leaps and bounds in the things of God. I can really see His hand in every hour and every event since that blessed hour with you. I am looking up, trusting, resting, enswathed in His presence!" He had found that which is fundamental.

God does not hand us a hymnbook and a volume of systematic theology and say, "Believe them and you will be saved." He offers us His Son, and says, "Believe in the Lord Jesus and you will be saved" (Acts 16:31 NLT). It is not an elaborate and orderly system of truths but "the truth," not a book of doctrines but a Person God offers us, and to whom He points us for salvation. "To all who believed him and accepted him, he gave the right to become children of God" (John 1:12 NLT).

It is not the acceptance of certain doctrines that saves the soul and gives it peace and purity and power, but a penitent and childlike faith in a divine Savior and loving loyalty to Him. And those who thus yield themselves up to Christ will have a revelation of Christ in their own souls. God will be unveiled to their understanding, and they will come to know that best and noblest of all knowledge, the knowledge of God and of Jesus Christ, which is life eternal. And then they will discover that they are not the first and only people to whom God has revealed Himself. They will find recorded God's revealings and unveilings of Himself through many ages to other penitent, trusting, loyally obedient, and chosen souls.

The Bible gives this record and becomes to them a living book. It interprets their own experiences to them, while their experiences with God help them to understand the Bible. They will further discover that wise and devout people—men and women of faith and prayer, students of the Bible and of religious experience—have gradually formulated and written down the things revealed in the Bible and in the experience of those who have come to know and walk with God. And these things are the doctrines, the articles of faith, the theology of those who believe them.

There is a sense in which all thoughtful, studious, prayerful Christians become their own theologians, working out under the leading of the Holy Spirit their own theology and discovering what they believe to be the true doctrines of the Bible. They may accept the teachings or doctrines of their parents and spiritual leaders, and hold them intellectually, but their theology is really limited to those articles of faith which vitalize their lives, guide and inspire their conduct, mold their spirits, comfort and guard their hearts, purify their natures, and kindle their hope for the future. It may be meager and quite inadequate to express and comprehend all that God has revealed in His Word to humanity, but it is all they have really made their very own. It will be a vast help to them, therefore, to find out what other devout people have discovered in the Word of God and have believed. It will enlarge, strengthen, confirm, and establish their faith and make it more intelligently their own. It will do them good, immeasurable good, to study and know the doctrines of the Bible and of their church. It will make them wiser, more steadfast and efficient, more full-orbed and luminous Christians.

The whole people of God for thousands of years have been laboring to grasp and make clear the teachings of God's Word, and the creeds of Christendom sum up the faith of the masterminds and devout spirits of the ages.

The importance and need of sound doctrine was never greater than now. Doctrinal preaching has very largely fallen into disuse. Family religion is neglected, and children grow up not knowing the faith of their fathers and mothers. People's minds are in a state of flux. Bold and blatant attacks are made upon the most sacred beliefs of God's people. Some declare conversion and regeneration to be the results of auto-suggestion.

Christ, according to some modern teaching, was a good man, but only a man—a psychologist who practiced hypnotism and so worked what were called miracles. Politically, according to the views of some, He was well to the left and, if He were living today, would lead a political and social revolution. He was not the Son of God, they assert, but the son of Joseph; not "the Lamb of God who takes away the sin of the world" (John 1:29 NLT) but a martyr to ideas that were in advance of His age but now well-known to every student of sociology and psychology.

The Bible has been described as a unique compilation of the folklore, scraps of history, myths, stories, songs, and religious literature of a Semitic tribe slowly emerging out of slavery and barbarism into civil and moral order and spiritual consciousness, but not a record of God's self-revealing. Such are some of the interpretations of the things so sacred and dear to our hearts which we and our children have heard.

Into this chilly, weltering sea of doctrinal confusion, evasion, and denial, let us boldly pour the warm stream of doctrinal assurance and certainty. Amid this Babel of anxious questionings and paralyzing doubts and bold denials, let us sound forth our proclamation of restful, assured, and well-reasoned faith.

The world needs a revival of faith in the truths and doctrines we have unwaveringly held from the beginning, which have nourished and comforted our souls and the souls of our fathers and mothers, firing them with quenchless zeal, making them more than conquerors on the hardest spiritual battlefields and fruitful in the most barren spiritual desert lands of earth. These doctrines find their sweetest and purest expression in our hymns and songs, their confirmation and incarnation in our holy and victorious lives, and their final affirmation and vindication on triumphant deathbeds.

These doctrines can be preached, and we ought to preach them. Doctrinal preaching need not be prosaic and dry as dust. It can be made thrillingly interesting by the use of illustrations, instructing and enlarging the understanding, kindling the affections, chastening the emotions, and purifying the heart. And it may be that one of the greatest services we can yet render to this and coming generations is to arrest the doctrinal drift of the times with a robust and reasonable faith, based on Scripture and confirmed by signs and wonders performed by the Holy Spirit in transformed lives.

NOTE

1. William Cullen Bryant, *Yale Book of American Verse*, ed. Thomas R. Lounsbury (New Haven: Yale University Press, 1912), 12.

The Miracle of Sustained Faith in Christ

I have a half brother who is an agnostic. After the death of our mother, when I was but a lad in my early teens and he was a little child of nine, we were separated. His father (my stepfather) took him south into the mountains of Arkansas, and later this boy went far west to the sounding shores of the Pacific while I went to the Atlantic seaboard. But we were not more widely separated in space than we became in faith. He is a man of the strictest integrity, clean living, high minded, honorable, and faithful in his friendships, and on several occasions he has been elected to positions of trust by his fellow citizens. But he is not a Christian.

I love him with a great and tender love. I have prayed with him and for him. Once he knelt at the penitent form in one of my meetings, and with all earnestness I have talked and written to him, but he remains an agnostic.

Recently he sent me an article clipped from a newspaper concerning an old clergyman in New York who, after fifty years, declared his unbelief in Christ and the Bible. My half brother seems to think that the apostasy of this old preacher is an argument against faith in Christ and the authority of the Bible.

But what is it that keeps faith in Jesus Christ alive century after century? People have been declaring their unbelief for ages. Ministers of the gospel have fallen from faith again and again. One of Jesus' own disciples betrayed Him, and the eleven remaining ones forsook Him in His hour of shame and death—yet people still believe in Him and prove their faith by transformed lives of utter self-sacrifice and lifelong devotion. What is the secret of this persistent faith? Is it in learned and subtle arguments? Is it what people have written in books that have kept this faith alive for two millennia? No, it is not these. It is not even the Bible records alone that constantly renew this faith.

There is but one thing that can account for it, and that is the ever-recurring revelation of Christ by the Spirit in penitent, obedient, believing souls. The ever-loving Christ coming to and abiding in hearts prepared and willing to receive Him keeps faith in Christ alive. We do not build our faith upon and sacrifice our lives for things people do not know or only half believe. In a court of law there may be a thousand people present who do not know anything about the case being tried, and no one cares to hear what they have to say; everyone is interested in what actual witnesses—who *do* have knowledge of the case—have to say.

Was Christ divine? Is He Lord? I do not know it only by what other people have said or written. Paul declared a great fact and principle when he wrote to the Corinthians, "No one can say Jesus is Lord, except by the Holy Spirit" (1 Cor. 12:3 NLT). This knowledge comes by revelation to each soul who will receive it. The Bible declares it, but until I get an experience that matches the Bible as a key fits a lock, I do not know it. I read the Bible for years. I taught it. I studied theology. I had books on the evidence for Christianity, and they seemed convincing to me, but I did not find the final and all-convincing evidence upon which I can anchor my soul in every storm and in the blackest night in those books; I found it in a personal revelation of Jesus Christ in my own heart. There was a glad sweet day when Christ revealed Himself within me. I could no more doubt this than I could doubt my own existence. My heart was filled with rapture. My soul was bathed in love. My eyes overflowed with tears of gratitude for His great love for me, and I sorrowed with a godly sorrow that I should ever have doubted or sinned against Him.

From that day, I was a transformed man. Worldly ambitions were swept away. Fleshly passions and tempers were mastered and subdued. Selfishness was lost in love, and if I had a thousand lives, each one would have been devoted to His service. And since that day I have been constantly witnessing this same transformation in other lives. I find my experience and the Bible constantly answering each other. They match each other as the key fits the lock. And it is this that keeps alive my faith in Christ. The Bible is the textbook showing how I may obtain this experience. When I obtain this experience, it confirms my faith in the Bible, while the Bible interprets my experience to me.

I remember kneeling in prayer with others for a young lady who was seeking the Savior as her Sanctifier. While we were praying, she suddenly burst into tears and exclaimed in a kind of rapture, "Oh Jesus!" and when she arose it was with a transfigured face. The light of heaven was upon her. Tears were in her eyes and there were rainbows in the tears. She had looked to Him and her face was radiant. She was beautiful. She was young and strong and well. All the full tides of youthful life were pulsing through her. But within six months, she was prepared to leave home and native land—and lover and friend—for Africa. She lived and labored and loved the people in the heart of the Congo country until one day her Lord said to her, "It is enough, come up higher," and she went to heaven by way of Africa. She said Christ had been revealed to her and within her.

I knew a man nearly forty years of age—educated, thoughtful, earnest—but without the knowledge of Christ in his heart. He took much offense at my testimony and for a year resisted me. Then, meeting another with a similar testimony, he came to me with great frankness and said, "In the mouths of two witnesses this thing is established. How can I get this revelation for myself?" I explained as fully as I could, and I told him to seek God with all his heart in obedient faith. One night he came to me and asked me to go with him to a meeting. I was not a Salvationist at the time, but I suggested going to The Salvation Army. When we arrived at the hall, everyone else was on the street conducting an open-air meeting.

We took a front seat, and soon I heard him whispering to himself. Turning, I found him with his elbow on the seat behind him, his face in his hand, and an upward look that was transfigured. He was whispering to himself, "Blessed Jesus, blessed Jesus!" I rejoiced, for I was sure the great revelation had come, and in my heart I prayed for him.

It is now nearly forty years since then, but I remember that prayer. It was one of the simplest prayers I ever prayed: "Oh Lord, bless him so that he will never get over it in this world or the world to come!" After the meeting began and the opportunity was given for testimonies, he stood and said, "No one can conceive what God has been doing in my soul this last half hour. Jesus Christ has come to my heart and revealed Himself within me." On the way home that night, he praised God almost every step of the way. The next night he came to my room and was still praising God. Everyone who knew him remarked at the transformation that had taken place in his life, in his looks, and in his words. He said that Christ was revealed to him and within him.

I knew an old man who had been an alcoholic for fifty-two years. Born of alcoholic parents, he began to drink when he was a little child. He was nursed at his alcoholic mother's breast and cradled in his alcoholic parents' home. At seven years of age, he was found drunk in a saloon, and he continued to drink for decades. He went to prison for crimes committed while under the influence of strong drink. He had an eye punched out in a drunken brawl and a leg and several ribs broken in fights. He grew up in vice and ignorance, never learning to read until after he found Christ.

One Fourth of July, at the age of fifty-nine, he came in from the mountains to a little town in California to drink and fight and have what he called "a good time." After visiting a saloon or two, he came to the railway station and saw a Salvation Army officer couple (ministers), in full uniform, waiting for the train. He thought he would have some sport and, eyeing them up and down and noting their uniforms, he questioned, "And w-w-what b-b-baseball t-t-team d-d-do you b-b-belong to?" They told him they were Salvationists, and they said that he ought to give his heart to God. But the man replied, "God wouldn't have anything to do with me. I'm a drunkard. I'm a prison bird. I'm on the road to hell."

But they spoke kindly to him, telling him that he need not go to hell, that God loved him, Jesus had died to save him, and that he could be a good man and go to heaven if he would repent and believe. They did not call him names. They did not point out to him what he already knew—that he was a disgrace to himself and society. They said to him, "Brother, you can be saved, and you can be saved here and now." They got the poor, wretched fellow down on his knees, and when he arose a great transformation had begun. Christ was coming into that dark heart. From that day forward, he drank no more. He gave up tobacco and amended all his ways, and for fifteen years lived an earnest Christian life and then died rejoicing in God. He said Christ had revealed Himself to him and in him.

This revelation was Paul's secret. Proud, gifted, highly educated, he hated Christ. He persecuted the Christians. He condemned them to death. But one day he said, "It pleased God . . . to reveal his Son in me" (Gal. 1:15–16 KJV). From that day he was a transformed man and henceforth gladly endured whippings; stonings and imprisonments; hunger and cold; weariness and pain; and innumerable perils on land and sea, in the country, and among enemies and false brothers. At last in prison, in sight of the executioner's block, when his head was to be cut off, he wrote triumphantly, "I have kept the faith" (2 Tim. 4:7 KJV). "We are more than conquerors through him that loved us" (Rom. 8:37 KJV).

This was the secret of Augustine, the brilliant but licentious young rhetorician of Carthage and Milan. The whole tide of his life was turned from sin to holiness, from impurity to purity, from deeds of darkness to light, and he said that Christ was revealed to him and in him.

Lord Tennyson was one day walking with a friend who asked him what he thought of Christ. The poet-philosopher and profound thinker was silent for a while. Then, stooping, he plucked a little flower and, holding it before him for a moment, said in his deep voice, "What the sun in heaven is to this little flower, that Jesus Christ is to my soul."

> I found Him not in world or sun,
> Or eagle's wing, or insect's eye;
> Nor thro' the questions men may try,
> The petty cobwebs we have spun:
>
> If e'er when faith had fall'n asleep,
> I heard a voice, "Believe no more,"
> And heard an ever-breaking shore
> That tumbled in the Godless deep,
>
> A warmth within the breast would melt
> The freezing reason's colder part,
> And like a man in wrath the heart
> Stood up and answer'd, "I have felt."
>
> No, like a child in doubt and fear:
> But that blind clamour made me wise;
> Then was I as a child that cries,
> But crying, knows his father near;

> And what I am beheld again
>
> What is, and no man understands;
>
> And out of darkness came the hands
>
> That reach thro' nature, moulding men.[1]

So wrote Tennyson in "In Memoriam." And in his poem "The Two Voices," he finds doubt over-mastered by what he calls "that heat of inward evidence."[2]

William E. Gladstone (whom many reckon to have been the greatest of all English statesmen) was a devout and humble Christian. In reply to a question about his Christian belief, he wrote, "All I think, all I hope, all I write, all I live for, is based upon the divinity of Jesus Christ, the central joy of my poor, wayward life."[3] On another occasion, he said, "If asked what is the remedy for the deepest sorrows of the human heart—what a man should chiefly look to in his progress through life as the power that is to sustain him under trials and enable him manfully to confront his afflictions—I must point him to something which, in a well-known hymn is called, 'The old, old story,' told of in an old, old book, and taught with an old, old teaching, which is the greatest and best gift ever given to mankind."[4]

If only one soul in the whole world has this revelation of Christ within, then faith in Christ is not dead and cannot die. But while there are millions who do not believe and who imagine that their unbelief will gradually cover the earth as the waters of the deluge once covered it in olden days, yet there are other millions whose hearts are full of praise, worship, and utter devotion to the dear Son of God who died for them. And this devotion—this tender, patient love, this constant faith—does not spring from what they have read in books, but is something that has come down from His heart to theirs through the eternal Spirit, when with penitential tears they have renounced sin and yielded their hearts to Him in simple, obedient trust as Savior and Lord. Then, to their awed, adoring, wondering souls He has revealed Himself within. And henceforth they believe with "that heat of inward evidence" to which nothing can be added until in the world to come they see Him face-to-face.

The Bible tells us how each of us may get this revelation for ourselves, and millions upon millions testify that—humbly and faithfully following these directions—they have received the great revelation. Let doubters doubt, let deniers deny, but all who will may prove it so—and this I have done. And all who will may prove it for themselves. I cannot prove to you that an article of food is sweet or sour; you must taste and see for yourself. So the psalmist says, "Taste and see that the LORD is good" (Ps. 34:8 KJV).

Faith in Christ is more than intellectual assent. It is a vital, throbbing, transforming moral assent that carries the soul into experiential fellowship and union with Christ. "Anyone who wants to do the will of God will know whether my teaching is from God or is merely my own," Jesus said (John 7:17 NLT). And again, He said, "If you love me, obey my commandments. And I will ask the Father, and he will give you another Advocate. . . . [And] you will know that I am in my Father, and you are in me, and I am in you" (John 14:15–16, 20 NLT).

My half brother—and every uncertain man or woman—can *know* when he is prepared to *do* His will and *obey* His commandments. There is a simple way to test whether a wire is dead or alive. Touch it. So there is a simple way to prove whether or not Jesus Christ is Lord. Do what He bids. Keep His commandments, "and his commandments are not burdensome" (1 John 5:3 NLT).

NOTES

1. Alfred Lord Tennyson, "In Memoriam," 1849, public domain.

2. Alfred Lord Tennyson, "The Two Voices," 1842, public domain.

3. William Gladstone, quoted in *The Literary World*, no. 29 (May 28, 1898): 169.

4. William E. Gladstone, quoted in *Bible Society Record*, no. 35 (1890): 11.

Paul's Secret: Alive in Christ   8

Among the grimmest words in the Bible are those of the risen Jesus to John on Patmos: "Write this letter to the angel [shall we say pastor?] of the church in Sardis. This is the message. . . . I know all the things you do, and that you have a reputation for being alive—but you are dead" (Rev. 3:1 NLT).

A dead shepherd of the sheep. A dead watchman of the city. A dead teacher of the unlearned. A dead nurse of little children. A dead physician of souls. A dead ambassador of heaven. *Dead!* Moving about, but dead. Occupying an important place, and so excluding any other who might fulfill its functions, but dead. Having the reputation of being alive, but dead. What could be sadder? What could be so ghastly?

But in contrast to this spiritually dead preacher was Paul. He was alive, all alive—throbbing, pulsing, overflowing with life—full of life divine, eternal. The most conspicuous among all Paul's wonderful traits was his robust, abounding spiritual life.

"This is eternal life," said Jesus, "that they may know You, the only true God, and Jesus Christ whom You have sent" (John 17:3 NKJV). If this is life, and life eternal, then Paul had it. The psalmist wrote of the wicked, "God is not in all his thoughts" (Ps. 10:4 KJV); but God was in all of Paul's thoughts. Paul knew God. "God, whose I am, and whom I serve," he said on the deck of a doomed ship (Acts 27:23 KJV). Paul knew Jesus Christ whom God had sent. Christ filled the whole heaven of Paul's soul. Eleven times he mentions Christ by name in the first chapter of Ephesians, and about every verse enshrines his Lord.

That is the great wonder of Paul's letters: they enshrine and enthrone Christ. Cut out the name of Jesus and His titles and the pronouns referring to Him, and you would so mutilate every chapter and nearly every verse in Paul's letters as to make them wholly unintelligible. Christ was his meat and Christ was his drink. He lived by Christ. He lived for Christ. He lived in Christ, and Christ lived in him. He lived Christ. Listen: "My old self has been crucified with Christ. It is no longer I who live, but Christ lives in me. So I live in this earthly body by trusting in the Son of God, who loved me and gave himself for me" (Gal. 2:20 NLT). And again he wrote, "For to me to live is Christ" (Phil. 1:21 KJV). How heartily—with what spirit and understanding—Paul would have sung some of our songs. How I would love to hear him and his companions sing:

﬩ My heart is fixed, eternal God,
Fixed on Thee, fixed on Thee;
And my unchanging choice is made,
Christ for me, Christ for me;
He is my prophet, priest, and king,
Who did for me salvation bring,
And while I've breath I mean to sing,
Christ for me, Christ for me.[1]

With what full and deep-toned fervor, with what exultant joy and star-like eyes and shining faces they would sing:

Christ is my meat, Christ is my drink,
My medicine and health,
My peace, my strength, my joy, my crown,
My glory and my wealth.

Christ is my father and my friend,
My brother and my love;
My head, my hope, my counselor,
My advocate above.

My Christ, He is the Heaven of heavens,
My Christ what shall I call?
My Christ is first, my Christ is last,
My Christ is all in all.[2]

Paul was no pillar saint, no Simon Stylites, no cloistered mystic sitting in rapt ecstasies or singing himself away to everlasting bliss in emotional spiritual songs. His heart was in heaven, his affections were there, but his feet resolutely trod the rough roads of earth and his hands grappled with its rough work. All the while his head planned campaigns for the conquest of earth's enthroned evils and cruelties and tyrannies, and for the healing of its foul diseases and festering sores. But in all his travels he had one single thought—to carry Christ to the people sitting in darkness and in the shadow of death. And in all his labors he had but one purpose—to make Christ known. In all his plans for spiritual conquest he had only one aim—to enthrone Christ in the faith and affections of others. He knew Jesus, and he knew that only Jesus could dispel the darkness in which the people sat and remove their fear of death by bringing them the life that is eternal. He knew that Jesus is the Friend and Brother of the toiler and that He can make all labor sweet. He knew that only Christ can overthrow entrenched evils and heal the deadly disease of sin by enthroning His Spirit in the human heart.

Let us note some of the evidence of life eternal in Paul, and so learn how more accurately to engage our own spiritual lives and how to nourish them. Nothing can be more important to us than this, whether as individuals or leaders, or more vital to the cause we serve and represent.

This life was manifest in Paul's spiritual appetites, just as all life is made manifest in its appetites. Paul hungered and thirsted after God. Hunger and thirst are two appetites that are inseparable from life—all life. When we cease to hunger and thirst, we are either sick or dead.

The more robust the life, the finer and firmer the health, the keener the appetite and more imperious the hunger and thirst will be.

Paul's hunger and thirst for God were insatiable. He drank and drank again, and yet he still was dry. He could have said with the psalmist, "As the deer longs for streams of water, so I long for you, O God. I thirst for God, the living God" (Ps. 42:1–2 NLT). Or he could have sung with Charles Wesley:

> I thirst for a life-giving God,
> A God that on Calvary died;
> A fountain of water and blood,
> Which gushed from Immanuel's side!
> I gasp for the stream of Thy love,
> The spirit of rapture unknown,
> And then to redrink it above,
> Eternally fresh from the throne.[3]

He was always reaching out after God, counting the dearest things as loss and rubbish that he might know Christ and win Him. Like a strong, determined runner, he pressed "toward the mark for the prize of the high calling of God in Christ Jesus" (Phil. 3:14 KJV).

This life was manifest in Paul's spiritual sensitivity. Not only was Paul's spiritual appetite keen, but all his spiritual senses were alive and wide awake. The soul has some senses that correspond to the senses of the body. Isaiah complained of those who had eyes to see but saw not, and ears to hear but heard not (see Isa. 6:9; 42:20). Jesus said repeatedly, "He who has ears to hear, let him hear!" (Matt. 11:15 NKJV). And when

He found the hearts of His disciples hardened by unbelief, He reproached them: "You have eyes—can't you see? You have ears—can't you hear?" (Mark 8:18 NLT). And the writer to the Hebrews mentions "those who by reason of use have their senses exercised to discern both good and evil" (Heb. 5:14 KJV).

It is this openness of spiritual senses that makes and characterizes spiritual leaders. Spiritual leaders are those who live in the Spirit, who dwell in such constant and intimate closeness with God that they and their Lord commune with each other, giving and receiving messages. They have such confidence in the report of their spiritual senses that when God gives them a vision, they are not disobedient to it. When God speaks, they rise up and follow. They know their Shepherd's voice, and that voice leads them on. Jesus said, "My sheep hear my voice, and I know them, and they follow me . . . [and] a stranger will they not follow, but will flee from him: for they know not the voice of strangers" (John 10:5, 27 KJV).

The modern physiologist who is sure that there is a sufficient material explanation for all the phenomena of mind and spirit, conscience and will—as well as of matter—would say it was no divine voice, but only the explosion of some overwrought brain cell or the erratic or unexplored activity of one of the endocrine glands. The devotee of the new psychology would have some other so-called scientific explanation that would exclude God. But the follower of Jesus can say with Paul, "I know whom I have believed" (2 Tim. 1:12 KJV) and assert that it is the voice of the Good Shepherd who goes before His sheep, while the sweetness and strength of their lives, and the glory and triumph of their martyrdoms, prove the truth of their confident assertion:

Where one heard noise, and one saw flame,

I only knew He named my name.[4]

It was the divine messages she heard and obeyed, and the spiritual
visions he saw and followed, that made William and Catherine Booth
the founders of The Salvation Army. It was the word sounding in the
depths of his soul, "The just shall live by faith" (Rom. 1:17 KJV), that
liberated Martin Luther. It was the word of the Lord in his own heart
that sent Livingstone to what was then referred to as "darkest Africa,"
and the vision of its awful darkness, shot through by the light of the
cross, held him there through long and painful years, until on his knees
he died praying for its redemption. It is the vision and the voice that
has called men and women from mines and mills and farms and
schools into Salvation Army ministry, and sent them to the four corners of the earth to be saviors of the lost. And it is the vision and the
voice still appealing to the seeing eye, the listening ear, and the understanding heart that can qualify and sustain us as spiritual leaders.

Paul's spiritual senses were not dead or dull, but alive, alert, and
in constant use. His spiritual ears were open; he heard voices and
received divine messages. His spiritual eyes were open; he saw heavenly visions and was not disobedient. His spiritual sensibilities were
alive; he had intense feelings.

His spiritual ears were open. "The Sovereign LORD has spoken to
me, and I have listened," wrote Isaiah. "Morning by morning he wak-
ens me and opens my understanding to his will" (Isa. 50:4–5 NLT).
And so Paul's ears were awakened. He had ears to hear, and he heard.
Christ spoke to him in the great crises of his life and ministry, and his

life and ministry were almost a continual crisis. A voice was always speaking in night visions or whispering in seasons of communion to reassure and guide him. On his way to Damascus, blinded by a sudden and great light from heaven, he heard a voice saying, "'Saul! Saul! why are you persecuting Me? . . . I am Jesus, whom you are persecuting. It is hard for you to kick against the goads'" (Acts 9:4–5 NKJV).

And in his defense before King Agrippa, Paul told us more that was then said to him:

 Now get to your feet! For I have appeared to you to appoint you as my servant and witness. Tell people that you have seen me, and tell them what I will show you in the future. And I will rescue you from both your own people and the Gentiles. Yes, I am sending you to the Gentiles to open their eyes, so they may turn from darkness to light and from the power of Satan to God. Then they will receive forgiveness for their sins and be given a place among God's people, who are set apart by faith in me. (Acts 26:16–18 NLT)

That was Paul's call to the ministry, his mighty ordination by the laying on of the pierced hands. What could quench the zeal of a man in whose soul was sounding such a message? And that was merely the beginning of messages from Jesus to Paul.

One night in Corinth, as Paul was beset by sleepless enemies and possibly battling with doubts and fears, the Lord appeared and spoke to him in a vision: "Don't be afraid! Speak out! Don't be silent! For I am with you, and no one will attack and harm you, for many people in this city belong to me" (Acts 18:9–10 NLT).

In his farewell address to the Ephesian elders at Miletus, Paul said, "And now I am bound by the Spirit to go to Jerusalem. I don't know what awaits me, except that the Holy Spirit tells me in city after city that jail and suffering lie ahead" (Acts 20:22–23 NLT). What a message! But it did not dampen Paul's ardor. His Lord, who had died for his sins, was marking out his way and going on before, and Paul followed without a whimper of self-pity or complaint or a moment's hesitation. He was very eager to go to Rome and preach the gospel there in the very center of the world's pride and pomp and power, but in Jerusalem he was arrested and held in prison for two years while enemies plotted against him. All his plans and hopes seemed finally and hopelessly blasted. But one night, as he lay in prison, the Lord stood by him and said, "Be encouraged, Paul. Just as you have been a witness to me here in Jerusalem, you must preach the Good News in Rome as well" (Acts 23:11 NLT).

And soon he was on his way to Rome with all passage money paid by the government, for he went as a prisoner and in chains. But to Rome he was going, and before Caesar he was to bear testimony to his Lord and plant saints in Caesar's household. But Paul was not only "bound in the bundle of life with the LORD" (1 Sam. 25:29 KJV), he was also bound in the common bundle of life with all of humanity, and he was not immune from any woe, disaster, sorrow, or sore amazement that might befall them. He was not the pet of Providence. His Lord did not shield him from hard blows, but comforted and strengthened him to bear them not only with patience, but also with joy.

He was on his way to Rome, but one day he and his fellow travelers found themselves caught in the grip of the sailor's dread, the tempestuous wind called Euroclydon. And for many weary nights and days they were tempest tossed, until one night all hope that they might be saved was taken away. What then were Paul's thoughts? Did doubts assail him? Did he wonder and question the revelation that he should go to Rome? He was a man with a nature like ours; he had the same temptations and was assailed by the same spiritual enemies. We can only guess what his thoughts were and the spiritual bewilderment and distress he may have been in as he lay wide awake that night when hope was taken away. But then the angel of God stood by him, saying, "Don't be afraid, Paul, for you will surely stand trial before Caesar! What's more, God in his goodness has granted safety to everyone sailing with you" (Acts 27:24 NLT). Paul believed, and was so assured that by his own cheerful countenance he lifted the hearts and hopes of the two hundred and seventy-six hopeless men on board and practically took command of the ship.

Tennyson might have had Paul in mind when he wrote, "Well roars the storm to those that hear a deeper voice across the storm."[5] One day Paul was praying for the third time for deliverance from a tormenting bodily affliction, "a thorn in the flesh," when he heard the voice of his Lord whispering, "My grace is sufficient for you, for my power is made perfect in weakness" (2 Cor. 12:9 ESV). In other words, "No, Paul, I will not remove the thorn, but I will give you grace to endure, to conquer in spite of it; and when people see you radiant and triumphant in your weakness, then they will confess the divinity in your life and give glory to Me." And Paul was so content with his Master's will, so eager to bring glory to Jesus, that he blessed that thorn and cried out, "Therefore I will boast all the more gladly of my weaknesses, so that the power of Christ may rest upon me. For the sake of Christ, then, I am content with weaknesses, insults, hardships, persecutions, and calamities. For when I am weak, then I am strong" (2 Cor. 12:9–10 ESV).

On another day he was praying and communing with his Lord, when suddenly he found himself caught up into some ineffable fellowship. He says it was the third heaven, where he heard words not lawful, not possible, to utter. Paul was alive in Christ. He had ears to hear and he heard. He had eyes to see and he saw.

The divine life was manifested through his activities. He worked harder than all others (see 2 Cor. 11:23). From city to city, continent to continent, on land and on sea, he went, carrying the message of a crucified, risen, coming Savior. The only rest he got was in prison, and there he won his guards and jailer to Christ. There he wrote some of the letters that comprise one-third of the New Testament and have blessed the world for two millennia—and will bless until time shall be no more.

The divine life in Paul was manifested in his quick sensibilities. When he saw injustice and wrong, he flamed with moral indignation. When he saw souls going down to doom, or Christians falling away from Christ, he wept. When he saw them turning to Christ, he exulted and rejoiced. For three years in Ephesus, he earned his own living by working at his trade of tent-making, and then by day and night as he had opportunity he visited from house to house and warned people with tears (see Acts 20:31). He wept with those who wept and rejoiced with those who rejoiced. With new followers of Jesus, he was gentle as a nurse with a little child, and he so loved them that he said he would gladly give his own life for them.

The divine life in him was manifested by its power. He stirred up bitter opposition, so bitter that his enemies were continually seeking to kill him, and once when they thought they had succeeded, they dragged him out and threw him on the city's garbage pile. But this life in him also kindled flaming, sacrificial love. No one was ever more deeply and tenderly loved than Paul. The Galatians would have plucked out their eyes and given them to him. Priscilla and Aquila offered their own necks for him.

The divine life in him brought dead souls to life. Onesimus, a run-away slave who had probably seen and heard Paul in his master's house, found the apostle in a Roman prison, became a follower of Jesus, and was sent back to his master. The church in Corinth was founded by Paul and its members—among whom were those who had been sexually immoral, idolaters, adulterers, homosexuals, thieves, greedy, drunkards, revilers, swindlers, a cross-section of the age—were his converts. Dead souls came to life when Paul touched them. Jesus said, "Have faith in me, and you will have life-giving water flowing from deep inside you" (John 7:38 CEV). Such rivers flowed from Paul, like the holy river seen by Ezekiel, healing, life-giving: "Life will flourish wherever this water flows" (Ezek. 47:9 NLT).

Finally, the divine life in Paul was manifested in his triumph over circumstances. They threw him into prison, and the jailer became a follower of Jesus. They stoned him and threw him on a pile of city refuse, giving him up for dead; but by and by, with a deep sigh, a gasp, and a struggle, he arose and went back to the city to comfort the disciples, and then passed on to other scenes of labor and suffering. Three times the Romans beat him with rods. Five times the religious authorities stripped his back bare and beat him with thirty-nine stripes—all the law would allow. Three times he suffered shipwreck. For a night and a day he clung to a spar of a wrecked ship while the wild waters raged and threatened to engulf him. He was hungry and cold, naked and thirsty, while salt waters billowed around him. His own countrymen slandered him. False brothers betrayed him. Robbers in the Macedonian hills and the Cilician mountains made his journeys dangerous. His life was so constantly endangered that he said, "I die daily" (1 Cor. 15:31 KJV). But his face was calm and radiant. He was not embittered or daunted. He was full of courage and deep and quiet peace which often leaped up into exultant joy. He gloried in his tribulations. I ask him, "Paul, Paul, how did you endure it all? What, oh what, is your secret? Tell me." And he replies, "I was less than the least of all saints. I was not worthy to be called an apostle. I was a 'blasphemer, persecutor, and insolent opponent' of the faith [1 Tim. 1:13 ESV], but I obtained mercy. The grace of our Lord was exceedingly abundant with faith and love. I am the chief of sinners. 'But God had mercy on me so that Christ Jesus could use me as a prime example of his great patience with even the worst sinners. Then others will realize that they, too, can believe in him and receive eternal life' [1 Tim. 1:16 NLT]. Christ died for me, and now the love of Christ constrains me, and I rejoice in my sufferings, as I participate in the continuing sufferings of Christ for His body, the church. My whole secret is this: 'My old self has been crucified with Christ. It is no longer I who live, but Christ lives in me. So I live in this earthly body by trusting in the Son of God, who loved me and gave himself for me' [Gal. 2:20 NLT]."

What a life! What an age-long, worldwide influence! He may tower immeasurably above us, but we have his secret. We can share the life that was his and exert some of that heavenly influence, if we are not dead while having a reputation for being alive.

NOTES

1. Richard Jukes, "My Heart Is Fixed, Eternal God," 1862, public domain.

2. John Mason, "I've Found the Pearl of Greatest Price," 1683, public domain.

3. Charles Wesley, "What Now Is My Object and Aim?" 1761, public domain.

4. Robert Browning, "Christmas Eve," 1850, public domain.

5. Alfred Lord Tennyson, "In Memoriam," 1849, public domain.

The Detachment of the Resurrection Life

The Chicago Post, a secular newspaper, in discussing a popular novel, refers to "the cry for light" by the book's hero, and says,

> The authentic note of the human soul rings poignantly in that cry. It is both incitement and appeal. Can that cry be answered? Yes, but not by weak compromise [and] not by abandoning the high demands of the cross for the pliant policy of "everything goes well, and everything is all right!" That sort of religion for a time may get glad hands, but it will never make glad hearts. Yes, there is light, and those who have seen its radiance must make it their task to remove the obscuring screens and let it shine, "The light of the knowledge of the glory of God in the face of Jesus Christ," as Paul calls it. That is the light of the world.[1]

The glory of God is seen in the face of Jesus Christ, and the knowledge of that glory alone can enlighten the world, dispelling its darkness, conquering its slavish fears, destroying its subtle sins and giant evils, and turning it once more into the Eden that was lost through disobedience.

This is our great task—so to live and love and labor as to unveil the face of Jesus Christ, and to let the world see the glory of God—the glory of His sacrificial love, atoning blood, sympathy, care, mercy, justice, and truth. And this we can only do as we keep ourselves disentangled from the world, as was our Master.

No one ever mingled with sinners more freely than did Jesus, and yet we read that He was "holy, blameless, pure, set apart from sinners" (Heb. 7:26 NIV). He was in the world, but not of it. He was brother to everyone, but He "didn't trust them, because he knew all about people. No one needed to tell him about human nature, for he knew what was in each person's heart" (John 2:24–25 NLT). He mingled and ate and walked and talked with them—not declining their invitation but accepting their hospitality—yet kept Himself separate from them and so drew them after Him and upward with Him. He walked with them and yet went before them. He came down to them and yet was above them. He loved them, yearned over them, and longed for their friendship and fellowship, and yet He would not compromise with them.

The Pharisees and rulers were frankly perplexed and puzzled by Him, because He seemed to be unconscious of—or to ignore—all the generally accepted moral and social distinctions, and moved freely among all classes of the people regardless of their reputed character. If a Pharisee invited Him to dinner, He went to dinner with a Pharisee.

If a tax collector gave Him an invitation, He accepted the invitation of the tax collector. If a fallen woman washed His feet with her tears and wiped them with the flowing tresses of her hair, He did not rebuke her or shrink from her touch but gently defended her from her critics and declared her sins forgiven.

Jesus commended the Samaritan whom the Jews despised. He heeded the cry and healed the daughter of the Syrophoenician woman who was only a Gentile dog in the eyes of His countrymen. He was a brother to all. He was the universal friend "without partiality, and without hypocrisy" (James 3:17 KJV). And He maintained this all-embracing wideness of sympathy and this freedom of action by His detachments. He belonged to no party. He committed Himself to no one. Since He belonged to no restricted, oath-bound brotherhood, He could be everybody's brother. Since He belonged to no party, He looked upon all parties without prejudice, and with utter impartiality He could judge righteously. Only so He could draw all men and women to Him and save them. And only so can His disciples to whom He has committed that great and unfinished work can save them also.

The Devil, by subtle appeal, sought to entangle Jesus, but the Master chose the hard and slow but sure way of the cross and returned from the wilderness temptations "in the power of the Spirit" (Luke 4:14 KJV). And always the Spirit accompanies with power those—and only those—who, keeping themselves disentangled, follow Him wholly.

How insistent and subtle was the temptation to entangle Joseph in the social life and fleshly lusts of Egypt! But he kept himself separate, and through the shame and pain, and the hardship of prison, he rose to supreme power and leadership because God prospered him. How fearlessly and marvelously Daniel and his three friends cut their way through the meshes of the nets of Babylon that would have snared them, and stood free and more than conquerors amid the dangerous intrigues and jealousies and idolatries of the great city, until the king was convinced and constrained to declare their God to be the living God, who alone can deliver and whose kingdom can never be destroyed but shall abide world without end, steadfast forever.

"And darkness covered the deep waters," we read in the first chapter of Genesis. "Then God said, 'Let there be light,' and there was light. And God saw that the light was good. Then he separated the light from the darkness" (Gen. 1:2–4 NLT). In this we have not only the statement of a great cosmic fact, but also a parable of the divine division between spiritual light and darkness — between those who are born of God and those who are still in their sins. The unregenerate world is in darkness. We ourselves "at one time . . . were darkness," wrote Paul. We walked in darkness, and the darkness blinded our eyes. "But now [we] are light in the Lord," he wrote (Eph. 5:8 ESV). But now we are "all children of the light and of the day; we don't belong to darkness and night" (1 Thess. 5:5 NLT). We have been called "out of the darkness into his wonderful light" (1 Pet. 2:9 NLT), and we are bidden to live as children of the light.

But as it was said of Jesus, so it is today: "The light shines in the darkness, and the darkness did not comprehend it" (John 1:5 NKJV). Unregenerate men and women cannot understand our aloofness. They are mystified by the austerity of God's people. They "are surprised that you do not join them in their reckless, wild living" (1 Pet. 4:4 NIV), that we are not prepared to join with them in their feasts.

The world offers its friendship to the saints, but on its own terms. The Devil promised Jesus the kingdoms of the world if He would fall down and worship Satan. And so we are promised ease and success, riches, popularity, and dominion, but only on terms of the world for its own ends. Wherever the children of God have been seduced by the world's glitter and flattery, and accepted its offers and entered into alliance with it, spiritual decay has begun, quick discernment of the Spirit and sensitivity of conscience has been lost, the spiritual appetite for prayer, Bible reading, and soul-winning has become dulled and sickly, and spiritual vision has blurred.

The Bible is full of examples illustrating this fact, and the history of the church from the days when church and state were wedded together by Constantine is replete with examples of such decadence. But every great spiritual movement—the Reformation, the rise of Puritanism, the Quakers, Methodism, and The Salvation Army among them, as well as every local revival—has been accompanied by a call for people who would be saved and purified and empowered by the Spirit to come out and be separate. Self-denial and cross-bearing are wholly inconsistent with worldly alliances and entanglements.

"How can light live with darkness?" asked Paul. "Come out from among unbelievers, and separate yourselves from them, says the LORD" (2 Cor. 6:14, 17 NLT). We must hold fast to that principle and steadfastly maintain that practice if we wish to retain spiritual power.

We must keep ourselves separate and disentangled for the sake of our freedom of action. We are soldiers, and true soldiers do not entangle themselves in business or social or political alliances, and they especially hold themselves aloof from embarrassing associations with the people with whom they are at war. We are ambassadors of Jesus Christ and of heaven, and however friendly ambassadors may be with the nation they represent, they must not for an instant allow themselves any association, however innocent it may appear, that may in any measure curtail their freedom of action in the interests of their own country.

We are kings and priests of God, like Nehemiah. We have a great work to do and all sorts of schemes, intrigues, and stratagems will be used to entangle us. Advisors will try to become controllers. Rich people will give us money on condition that they can have a veto on our freedom in the use of it. Political parties and fraternal organizations will be our friends but will insist on having a voice in our decisions.

We must maintain our freedom that our judgment may be unclouded and impartial. In Christ Jesus, Paul wrote, "there is not Greek and Jew, circumcised and uncircumcised, barbarian, Scythian, slave, free; but Christ is all, and in all" (Col. 3:11 ESV). If he were writing today I think he would say, "There is neither English nor Irish, German nor French, American nor Japanese, African nor Asian, Catholic nor Protestant, Muslim nor Jew, but Christ is all and in all." Jesus tasted death for everyone. "The arms of love that compass me would all the world embrace."[2] If we would walk in our Savior's footsteps, we must enter into no association and allow ourselves to become possessed of no party spirit that would cloud our judgment of any group and narrow the breadth of our sympathy or chill the ardor of our love for all humanity.

It was at this point that the ancient Jews—and especially the Pharisees—failed. They were God's chosen people. Through them the great revelation of God, of His character, mind, and will came. They were separated from all the peoples of the earth by divine command. But they forgot or failed to comprehend that this was for the purpose of so protecting them from degrading influences and of illuminating and instructing them that they might become a channel through which God could bless all the families of the earth. They failed to grasp the purpose of their separation.

God's thought was to protect and liberate them from enslaving idolatries, degrading superstitions, debasing lusts and orgies of passion, injustice, and pride and pomp and vaulting ambitions. But they fell into a pit of spiritual pride and became utterly narrow and bigoted, trusting in themselves that they were righteous and despising others. Through them God wanted to reveal and pour out the ocean of His redeeming love upon the whole world. But they failed Him. And so may we, if we do not keep ourselves—like our Master—"holy, blameless, pure, set apart from sinners" (Heb. 7:26 NIV), and at the same time keep our hearts full of "the wisdom from above [that] is first pure, then peaceable, gentle, open to reason, full of mercy and good fruits, impartial and sincere," sowing in peace the fruits of righteousness (James 3:17–18 ESV).

NOTES

1. Quoted in Howard Agnew Johnston, *Scientific Christian Thinking* (New York: George H. Doran Company, 1922), 224.

2. Charles Wesley, "Jesus! The Name High over All," 1749, public domain.

Redeeming the Time 10

What! So soon? Another year? Every January, it seems impossible that another year could have passed so swiftly. And yet the start of a new year assures me that once more the earth has run its wondrous race through lanes of light and vast voids of space and deep abysses of the night, amid the silent pomp and splendor of star-strewn heavens, completing another of its ceaseless cycles around the sun, ending another year.

Shortly thereafter, on January 9 each year, the passage of time also brings me to the anniversary of that glad hour when God sanctified my soul. I never cease to wonder at His loving-kindness and mercy when that day comes. "Let all that I am praise the LORD; with my whole heart, I will praise his holy name. Let all that I am praise the LORD; may I never forget the good things he does for me. He forgives all my sins and heals all my diseases. He redeems me from death and crowns me with love and tender mercies. He fills my life with good things. My youth is renewed like the eagle's!" (Ps. 103:1–5 NLT).

When I was a little boy on the sun-bathed prairies of southern Illinois, a year seemed interminable. It moved forward on leaden feet, but now the years pass me like the flash of sunlit bubbles on wind-tossed waves, as though they must hasten and lose themselves in that eternity when time shall be no more. And yet what an unspeakable gift of God is a year! Who can compute its value or estimate its worth? We give and receive our little gifts and rejoice, but how paltry they are compared to God's gift of a year of days!

He has given me one more year, and I praise Him. It has been a good year. He has crowded it with mercies. He has crowned it with blessings. He has kept me from sin. He has not permitted me to fall. He has not let my Enemy triumph over me. He has directed my paths and ordered my steps. He has given success to my labors. He has kept my heart and mind in peace, and in loving-kindness has opened to me the gates of another year, through which I enter with trust, and yet with trembling. I do not fear that I shall fall—though I know I must watch and pray lest I fall—but I trust unfalteringly that my watchful Keeper, my Good Shepherd, who has guarded me with such sleepless care through these many years, will hold me up.

I rejoice with the psalmist, who sang, "My help comes from the LORD, who made heaven and earth! He will not let you stumble; the one who watches over you will not slumber. . . . The LORD keeps you from all harm and watches over your life. The LORD keeps watch over you as you come and go, both now and forever" (Ps. 121:2–3, 7–8 NLT).

And yet I tremble at the solemn responsibility laid upon me in the gift of another year of days, lest I fill them up not as full of prayer and praise and useful service as I should. Paul wrote of "redeeming the time" (Eph. 5:16 KJV) or, rather, as the Greek text has it, "buying up the time, because the days are evil."

It is so easy to kill time—to let it slip through one's fingers like sands of the seashore, or to fritter it away doing some good thing, or *better* thing, instead of the *best* thing. One of the snares of this age is its exceeding busyness—and it is a snare set especially to trap the servants of God and ministers of the gospel. It makes us too busy to wait patiently on God in secret prayer, too busy to quietly read the Bible for personal soul food, too busy for meditation—and yet "blessed" people are those who "delight in the law of the LORD, meditating on it day and night" (Ps. 1:2 NLT). It makes us too busy to speak to others about their souls and lead them to the Savior, too busy to give time to self-examination and solemn, secret worship and adoration of the Lord. It makes us so busy about the Lord's work that God Himself is forgotten, or only dimly remembered, and crowded into the corner and background of our thoughts, affections, time, and work.

Oh, Lord, pluck our feet out of this net! Let us not fall into this pit dug for us by the Enemy of our souls! And yet how easy it is to redeem the time if we just rouse ourselves into spiritual wakefulness and set ourselves with quiet, steady purpose of heart to do so. "Let us not sleep, as others do," wrote Paul, "but let us keep awake and be sober" (1 Thess. 5:6 ESV).

A big policeman sat in front of me on the streetcar. He had just come in out of biting wind and bitter cold. As I rose to leave the car,

I laid my hand on his shoulder and said, "God bless you today!" He glanced up with surprise but with a look of gratitude, as though I had given him a cup of cold water on a hot and dusty day. And as I pressed my way out of the car, my own heart was refreshed. With one word, I had bought up that moment and redeemed so much time.

A poorly clad man stood irresolutely in the wintry wind on a busy street corner. As I passed him, I tapped him on the shoulder and said, "God bless you!" And as I looked back I saw his plain face light up as though a burst of sunlight had fallen upon it.

I sat at dinner in the home of a stranger, with three men and their wives. With a little watchfulness and without any effort, the conversation was turned to spiritual things, after which we prayed. Later one of the women remarked to one of the others, "I felt as though we were talking to God." And so we were—to God and about God and His gracious ways and work in the soul—and our hearts burned within us. So the time that might have been lost in profitless small talk was redeemed—bought up—and given to the Master.

I sat in the train, and taking my Bible I began to read. A vibrant voice from the other side of the car inquired, "You have something good there, haven't you?" I looked up into the clear eyes of a gray, but vigorous, strong-faced man. "Yes," I replied, "the Bible." And for hundreds of miles we rode and talked together about the things of God—the things that make for our eternal peace and welfare. I found him to be the lieutenant of one of the mightiest living financiers, burdened with great responsibilities and apparently glad to have someone to talk to him about the riches that shall not perish when the heavens have rolled together as a scroll and fled away, and the earth—with all therein—is burned up.

An elevator operator, once employed at our headquarters, used to redeem the time, and he won over sixty souls to Jesus among those he carried up and down in his elevator.

I asked a lady, who was rejoicing in the Lord, when she became a follower of Jesus. She asked me if I did not remember speaking to her on the streetcar about her soul, some months before. I did not remember. "Well," said she, "that set me thinking, and I found no rest till I found Jesus and knew I was born again."

I went to a Christian home one night. As I was being shown to my bedroom, I leaned over the stairway and asked my host if he was enjoying the blessing of a clean heart indwelt by the Holy Spirit. The next day at the dinner table I asked him again, and he promptly replied, "Yes. Your question last night made me see my need, and this morning in the office of my store, alone with God, I sought and found the blessing."

Many years ago in Nashua, New Hampshire, I asked permission of a lady in whose home I was being hosted to mark a text in her Bible. Years later we met in California, and she reminded me of it. She said, "An unbeliever came to our home after you left and was railing against God and religion. My Bible was lying open on the center table. He took it up. His eyes fell on that marked text, and it smote his heart and conscience. He fell under deep conviction and became a follower of Jesus as a result of that reading."

It is enough to make one weep and shout for joy to see how unfailingly God works with those who constantly and unselfishly and in faith work for Him.

"Be prepared, whether the time is favorable or not," wrote Paul to Timothy (2 Tim. 4:2 NLT). It is not always some great, conspicuous public effort that brings forth the most fruit to God's glory, but often the wayside word. It was not amid the thronging multitude of Jerusalem in the courts of the temple that Jesus started His greatest revival, but on the curb of a wayside well where He found a fallen woman and told her of the Living Water. Her heart was won, and she went to the city and kindled faith in the hearts of the people, until they came out in throngs to see and hear Jesus and the whole city was revived.

If we watch and pray, if we give heed to the movings of the Spirit within us, we shall find ourselves redeeming the time in the most unexpected and yet most effective ways. For it is the word that is unexpected, the word that seems "out of season" (2 Tim. 4:2 KJV), arresting the attention of the hearers and catching them off guard, that enables us to enter into the strong city of Mansoul before the gates can be shut to capture it for the Master. I have especially found, again and again, that a word spoken to a child will bring forth precious fruit. But thereon hangs a number of sweet stories I must write about at some other time.

Bless God for the year just closed, and bless God for the new, clean, inviting year stretching out before me! I welcome it! I throw my arms wide open to embrace it! It will have sunny days and cloudy days, but each will be the day the Lord has made. And my soul exults to run its race and fight its battle and score its triumphs in these coming days, for I expect triumph over every foe, victory over all enemies of my soul, and good success in all my labors this coming year.

He has said, "My presence will go with you, and I will give you rest" (Ex. 33:14 ESV). He has said, "Be sure of this: I am with you always, even to the end of the age" (Matt. 28:20 NLT). I believe, so how can I fail to be victorious? Why should I not exult and be glad? Why should I not be strong in the Lord and in the power of His might? What more can He say than all He has said to encourage my faith? Why should I not believe? I *will* believe, I do believe and, believing, I have peace—perfect peace—and so go forth in full confidence of victory every day.

I invite you to join me in a covenant of faith to live this year with and for God, redeeming the time!

> I would the precious time redeem,
> And longer live for this alone,
> To spend and to be spent for them
> Who have not yet my Savior known;
> Fully on these my mission prove,
> And only breathe, to breathe Thy love.

> My talents, gifts, and graces, Lord,
> Into Thy blessed hands receive;
> And let me live to preach Thy Word,
> And let me to Thy glory live;
> My every sacred moment spend
> In publishing the sinner's Friend.

> Enlarge, inflame, and fill my heart
> With boundless charity divine,
> So shall I all strength exert,
> And love them with a zeal like Thine,

And lead them to Thy open side,

The sheep for whom the Shepherd died.[1]

NOTE

1. Charles Wesley, "Give Me the Faith Which Can Remove," 1749, public domain.

Go for Souls—and Remember Your Allies

11

A troupe of theatrical people filled (with the exception of another gentleman and myself) the sleeper car in which I was to cross New Mexico on a recent journey. The girls of the theatrical troupe were pretty, painted little things, with penciled eyebrows and lashes, and bizarre dresses. And, of course, they were friendly with all the men of the party—yet not in a bold way to arouse suspicion that they were bad. They were just frivolous and void of all apparent seriousness.

My heart was a bit heavy and cast down when I looked at them and listened to their empty chatter. There was nothing in common between us, it seemed to me, but I found my heart going out with pity and sympathy toward the young things who seemed so pathetic in their spiritual poverty and ignorance of all the high and true and lasting values of life.

When the porter began to make up the berth for the night, one of the older girls, waiting, sat on the arm of one of the seats of my berth.

I removed my coat from the seat and begged her to sit down. She hesitated—possibly she felt the lack of common interest as much as I, for she saw me in full Salvation Army uniform—but then sat with me. For a few moments we sat opposite each other in silence while she watched in rather a grave way what appeared to be a furious flirtation going on across the aisle.

I wanted to speak to her but hardly knew how to begin. At last, however, I made some commonplace remark about the weird desert through which we were passing—the indescribably wild, bare mountains flooded and glorified by the transfiguring light of the setting sun which rimmed the desert in—and soon we were in conversation. I asked her about her work, and she told me of the long hours they spent in play and rehearsal—from ten to twelve hours every day—a matinee in the afternoon, and play again from 7:30 to 11:30 p.m., never getting to bed before 1 a.m. I noticed that beneath the camouflage of paint and powder and wild profusion of golden hair she looked tired and, I thought, a bit world-weary and disappointed. I asked her if she didn't miss home life, and she told me she had a good home in Chicago, but that she got restless after spending two or three weeks there and then must go on the road again.

I told her that I understood, that I was sure that this restlessness would grow and become more and more consuming, and that I knew of just one cure—that of which old St. Augustine wrote: "Thou, O God, hast made us for Thyself, and we are restless till we rest in Thee."[1] I told her that our souls were too great to be satisfied with anything less than God Himself, and that He is the rightful home and great Friend of the soul. I told her that when I was a little orphan boy, through the death of my father, it was not the four walls of the house where Mother and I lived that made my home, but Mother herself. She was the home of my little child-soul. But by and by she, too, died, and then my soul found its true rest and rightful home in God, in fellowship and union and sweet and tender friendship with Him.

I told her of Jesus and His great love and sacrifice for us all, and she listened—oh, so quietly and intently—and then she arose and gave me her hand in an eager and warm clasp. Then, looking deep into my eyes, thanked me with an earnestness that made me forget the paint and powder—for her soul was looking directly at mine—and then she was gone. But an indescribable sweetness filled my heart. I felt Jesus' presence, as when He was upon earth, still seeking the lost to save them. And then I realized, it seemed as never before, how He was the Friend of sinners, how He loved them and longed for them. And that night He gave me a fresh baptism of love for the lost and wayward, the straying, and the befooled souls who are trying to find satisfaction without Him.

At three o'clock in the morning, in the stillness and darkness, that weary troupe of players slipped out of the train so silently that I did not hear them go, and I may never see them again. But my soul has been sweetened by the chance meeting with them. The quiet talk with the girl who is beginning to be disillusioned and to feel the vanity of all things without Christ, left a blessing in my soul that will abide, and in the strength of that I shall go for many days.

William Booth, The Salvation Army's founder, called us to "Go for souls!" Souls! They are all about us. We move among them and through the pulsing, throbbing midst of them like a great ocean. They beat around us like the waves of the sea. They are ever with us. We cannot get away from them unless we flee to the wilderness, and even there they will come to us. And if we, like our Lord, are the friends of sinners we shall not find them hard to approach. The difficulty is in ourselves rather than in them. We ourselves may be stiff and formal, hesitant, shy, and uncertain just what to say and how to begin. But I find that if I lift my heart to God in secret prayer for wisdom and words and love, the way opens and I can talk with almost anyone.

On that same sleeper car I talked to the porter, and he seemed most grateful that I should have thought enough of him to inquire about his soul. I found he was a Christian, and we had fellowship together.

People everywhere have open hearts to you, and it will be a rare thing for anyone to snub your coming in love, with a shining face and a warm heart full of real compassion and sympathy. Indeed, do they not expect you to speak to them? Let us not disappoint them. Let us deal with them boldly, kindly, tenderly, and faithfully, and Jesus will be with us and our hearts will surely burn with the sweetness of His presence and favor. He will be pleased with us as He sees us about His business, seeking the souls for whom He died.

There are difficulties in the way of reaching souls today. There is the drift away from organized religion. People do not care to go to religious services. The church is no longer attractive to masses of people. They much prefer to go shopping on Sundays or spend their evenings in the movie theaters. But we must not magnify this difficulty. In Paul's day the masses of people went to pagan temples and theaters. In Wesley's day they went hunting and to cockfights. And when William Booth began his work in London they thronged the streets and flooded the saloons. But those men of God compelled their attention, and so must we.

Yes, there is a decay of the sense of sin and the reverent fear of God among people today. But this is due to a failure to hear the whole counsel of God proclaimed by fire-touched lips and hearts aflame with the sense of God's claims and the danger of neglect. Let us get a fresh sense of sin's deadly character and the everlasting darkness and desolation into which it plunges human souls, and let us feel afresh "the terror of the Lord" (2 Cor. 5:11 KJV). Let us recall that apart from Christ He is a consuming fire (see Heb. 12:29), and we shall awaken hearts to a sense of sin and that reverent fear of God which is "the beginning of wisdom" (Prov. 9:10 KJV) and which leads men and women to "depart from evil" (Job 28:28 KJV).

Personally, I always carry with me in my heart the knowledge that God is love, and in my conscience the sense that "our God is a consuming fire" (Heb. 12:29 KJV). That knowledge casts out slavish fear, and that sense creates reverent fear, destroys trifling with sacred truths and duties, and makes me walk softly, lest I fall and become a castaway. Oh, that we may be so filled with the Spirit that we may arouse wholesome fear in the hearts of men and women, shake them out of their complacency, and make them realize how deeply they have grieved and offended God, how constantly and heartlessly they have sinned against infinite love and holiness, and how deadly is their peril unless they make haste to repent and find shelter in the wounds of Christ. But while we face difficulties in doing this, we also have allies.

The human heart is our ally. It is sinful and corrupt, but it was made for God, and is sad and restless and constantly subject to vexation, disappointments, and vague longings and fears until it finds God. And when we once succeed in interpreting to people this trouble in themselves, we have gone a long way to win them. This interpretation is made not only by what we say, but also by what we are—by the radiance and rest, peace and joy, earnestness and purity of our lives—and by the looks on our faces which reflect the blessedness that is resident in our hearts.

Human weakness is our ally. Human beings are weak and dependent—they must have help or perish. From the cradle to the grave, from birth to death, they are dependent upon others and upon God's unfailing fullness. Houses are built for them, clothes are made for them, food is produced for them, books are written for them, teachers are provided for them, laws are enacted to protect them, police are hired to defend them, highways and railroads and ships all around the world serve them and make possible the supply of their daily needs, the gospel is preached to save them—and behind it all is the heavenly Father pouring sunshine and rain upon them, without which they would perish. They come into the world as helpless babies, with a gasp and a cry, and they go out of the world just as helpless, with a gasp and a sigh. If we can make them feel this helpless dependence we have gone a long way toward winning them.

The human conscience is our ally. In every human heart, conscience sits in judgment upon a person's own acts, choices, and character. In the clamor and riot of passion, pleasure, and business, its voice may not be heard or heeded, but if we can silence the clamor by a song, a testimony, a word of God, till the still small voice of conscience is heard, we will have gone a long way. Conscience is God's ally and ours in every human heart.

Good Christian people are our allies. They may not come to our church to help us there, but they are helping to dispel the darkness that envelops those who are still lost in their sins. God hears their prayers, and they—maybe all unconsciously—are our helpers. We are not alone; there are seven thousand who have not bowed the knee to Baal (see 1 Kings 19:18). And we never know when they may so drive back the Enemy at their point in the far-flung battle line that it will make him an easy conquest in our particular sector. We are not alone in our warfare.

Deaths, funerals, and open graves are our allies. Through these, like landscapes lighted on dark nights by lightning flashes, men and women glimpse eternity, and its solemnities compass them round. God speaks and they must hear. Let us appeal to the realities of eternity and press them home with earnestness upon the attention of our hearers, and we shall go a long way toward winning them.

God the Holy Spirit is our ally. He is before and behind and all about us. He is ever whispering to people's hearts, striving with their wills, quickening their consciences, keeping alive the memory of their sins. Let us cooperate with Him, and work in glad and bold confidence, since He is our Helper. He will bring Calvary's scenes before us, if we wait on Him, and He will help us to make others see Jesus. He will help us to pray, believe, and win souls.

NOTE

1. St. Augustine, quoted in Rufus M. Jones, *Fundamental Ends of Life* (Whitefish, MT: Kessinger, 2003), 115.

Where Is Your Faith?

12

A timid little woman went "fishing"[1] in a prayer meeting one night and spoke to two young men about their souls, urging them to give their hearts to God. They were really interested but managed to appear unconcerned and amused. It was her first attempt at this practice and her faith failed. Instead of kindly and earnestly sticking to them, she went back to her seat and wept, feeling that she had done more harm than good. But God was not discouraged. He did not leave those young men.

That night in bed one of them woke up and found the other weeping. "What's the matter, Tom?"

"Oh, I feel I'm on the road to hell. That woman spoke to us kindly and we laughed in her face. I'm not fit to live. I wish I were saved."

"I wish I were, too, Tom."

They got out of bed and prayed until they found peace with God. The Holy Spirit was far more interested in those boys than that little woman was, and He was working with her. But she did not believe and so she got no comfort. But God's strength was made perfect in her weakness. He did not fail her because her faith failed. He remained true, though she doubted.

It is this faithfulness of God—His unchangeable goodness and love—that should make us strong and steady in faith. God's character is the ground of our faith and hope. His faithfulness is like the great mountains that stand unchanged through the storms of a thousand years. People who live among the mountains or by the ocean do not expect to wake up some morning and find the mountains vanished or the sea dried up. They may be hidden for a time by fog and cloud but the wise people still reckon that they are there.

Let us be wise concerning God. We should not be doubtful and fearful and downcast, but glad and radiant with the peace, joy, and strength that are born of faith in God, in His gracious, holy, changeless character.

For three years, Jesus was training a few stupid men to believe, so that they might reveal God to the world and turn it upside down. But they were slow to learn, and again and again He said, "O you of little faith" (Matt. 8:26 ESV); "Have you still no faith" (Mark 4:40 ESV); and "If you have faith" (Matt. 17:20 ESV).

His heart was hurt by their distrust. But oh, how glad He was when He found someone who believed, who trusted Him against all contrary appearances. One day a Gentile woman came to Him and cried to Him to cast out a demon from her daughter. "But Jesus gave her no reply, not even a word" (Matt. 15:23 NLT). His disciples were ashamed to have such a woman following and crying after Him along the streets, and urged Him to send her away. Then He said to them in her hearing, "I was sent only to help God's lost sheep—the people of Israel" (Matt. 15:24 NLT).

What hope was there for her after that? She was a Gentile and a woman. But she drew near and "worshiped him, pleading again, 'Lord, help me!'" Then for the first time He spoke to her: "It isn't right to take food from the children and throw it to the dogs" (Matt. 15:25–26 NLT).

What a trial of faith! But Jesus is not always easy with us. His fondness for us is not foolish. He does not hesitate to try us, and happy are we if our faith does not fail. There shall be a big reward.

This woman's faith did not fail. It rose above every difficulty. It triumphed over every objection. The scorn of the disciples and the seeming indifference of the Master merely increased the doggedness of her faith. She cried out, "That's true, Lord, but even dogs are allowed to eat the scraps that fall beneath their masters' table" (Matt. 15:27 NLT). She would take the dog's place. She would not doubt. She did not faint, but persisted in prayer.

At last Jesus had found one who really believed, and how glad He was. His great, yearning love was met by great faith, and His heart was satisfied. He answered, "Dear woman . . . your faith is great. Your request is granted" (Matt. 15:28 NLT). It was as though the Lord had said to her, "Help yourself. My treasure house is open to you. Take what you want." Faith had won. She could have all her heart's desire. "And her daughter was instantly healed" (Matt. 15:28 NLT).

True faith is the most wonderful thing in the world. With it a handful of ignorant Jewish fishermen and tax collectors turned the world upside down. It makes beggars act like kings, for they know they are children of the King. Though they are so poor that they don't know where they will get their next crust, and have no place to lay their heads, yet they sing, "I'm the child of a King. . . . A tent or a cottage, why should I care? They're building a palace for me over there."[2]

"Hasn't God chosen the poor in this world to be rich in faith?" wrote James (James 2:5 NLT).

Faith makes the sorrowful to rejoice. I saw a devoted young wife and mother, whose young husband had suddenly died, smile through her tears as she believed God. Her face was a benediction; it was like the rising of the sun on a cloudless morn. "As sorrowful, yet always rejoicing," wrote Paul (2 Cor. 6:10 ESV).

Faith lightens the load of the heavy-laden. Paul fairly reveled in this fact. He wrote to his friends and fellow Christians in Philippi, "I can do everything through Christ, who gives me strength" (Phil. 4:13 NLT).

What could have enabled William Booth to go on through the years of obscurity and scorn, opposition and poverty, and to have borne his immeasurable burden of care and responsibility, but faith in God? I have sometimes thought he must have had some inward spiritual secret that bore him up and on. But I am persuaded that his secret was the old secret of the saints and warriors of the Lord from Abraham until now. He "believed God" (Gal. 3:6 KJV). He counted on God, even when God, like the mountains, was hidden by clouds. And as he believed, he found that God was there.

Faith empowers one to do the impossible. Peter walked on the sea while he believed, and not until he doubted did the waves open their hungry mouths to swallow him up.

I know a young fellow who seemed to have no gifts or skill for winning souls, but through faith and faithful work he has become one of the most skillful soul-winners I know.

Faith may see difficulties, but it does not magnify them; it minimizes them. It takes no account of them. It rises above them. It has vision. It sees God. It looks at His power and love and resources, and casts itself on Him, and through Him it triumphs.

> Faith, mighty faith, the promise sees,
> And looks to that alone;
> Laughs at impossibilities,
> And cries: It shall be done![3]

Faith may be sore tempted, but it does not yield to discouragement. When we yield to discouragement, we at that moment cease to believe. We let our troubles get between us and God and shut Him out. They appear to be bigger than God, or at least bigger than any interest He has in us.

Doubt puts us behind our difficulties. The difficulties, then, hide God from us, and so we get discouraged. Faith puts us in front of our difficulties, on the Godward side of them, and in quietness and confidence we face them, assured that God is with us and will in His own way and time deliver us. It was so with Daniel and his three friends in Babylon, and it has been so with God's people from then until now.

Finally, faith obeys. It does not sit in dreamy idleness but works as it has opportunity. The disciples had toiled all night in fishing and caught nothing. Jesus, standing on the shore in the dawn, said to them,

"Go out where it is deeper, and let down your nets." Peter answered, "If you say so, I'll let the nets down again" (Luke 5:4–5 NLT). And he got such a multitude of fish as to break his net. He beckoned his partners, and they came and filled their little ships to the point of sinking. Peter was fairly embarrassed by the abundant fruit of his obedient faith. But real faith obeys where there is no sign.

Adoniram Judson, the first American missionary to Burma, which today is officially known as Myanmar, labored for seven years without anyone coming to faith in Christ. A friend wrote, asking him what the prospects were. He replied, "The prospects are as bright as the promises of God."[4] The promises are like the stars; the darker the night, the brighter they shine. Shortly after, Judson's faith was rewarded with thirty thousand new followers of Jesus. It is a wonderful thing to truly believe God, to keep a listening ear for His word, and a heart and hand ready to obey. Have faith in God.

NOTES

1. A practice of prayerfully discerning and approaching people who seem to be ready to respond to the Holy Spirit's prompting but may need encouragement to do so.

2. Harriet E. Buell, "A Child of the King," 1877, public domain.

3. Charles Wesley, "Father of Jesus Christ, My Lord," 1742, public domain.

4. David Shibley, *Great for God: Missionaries Who Changed the World* (Green Forest, AR: New Leaf Press, 2012), 49.

Red-Hot Religion 13

One of the unsolved problems of science is to produce a physical light that is cold. The problem we face is to produce a spiritual light that is hot—and that is none other than the old-time religion.

Jesus said of His forerunner, John the Baptist, "He was a burning and a shining light" (John 5:35 KJV). He shone until Jerusalem and Judea and all the regions around Jordan were startled and awakened by the light, and went out to see and to hear. And he burned into their hard, cold hearts until multitudes confessed their sins. King Herod himself and his adulterous wife were so scorched by the heat of the burning herald of righteousness that Herod shut John up in prison, and at the request of his dancing stepdaughter, urged on by his wicked wife, had John's head cut off to escape the burning, as though the loss of his head could quench the fire that shone and burned in John's heart and life.

Solomon said, "Wisdom lights up a person's face" (Eccl. 8:1 NLT). And the psalmist said, "Those who look to [the Lord] for help will be radiant with joy" (Ps. 34:5 NLT).

We read that when Moses came down from the mount where he had met with God, "the Israelites could not gaze at Moses' face because of its glory" (2 Cor. 3:7 ESV; see also Ex. 34:29–35). And we also read of Stephen, "Everyone in the high council stared at Stephen, because his face became as bright as an angel's" (Acts 6:15 NLT).

Some time ago a Chicago multimillionaire spoke at a Salvation Army meeting, and among other things said that the one thing that always most impressed him as he looked upon a company of Salvationists was the light in their faces. (May that light never go out!) This light is produced by that heavenly wisdom that comes from the knowledge of God through faith in Jesus, and by the peace of a good conscience and love to all.

But those who most mightily move men and women to righteousness are not only shining, but also burning lights. John burned his way into the dulled consciences of the people of his day and stirred all Judea and Galilee. Stephen burned into the guilty souls of priests and rulers until their wrath knew no bounds, and they cast him out and sent him to heaven in a shower of stones. The apostles burned their way into idolatrous cities and into a pagan civilization reeking with unmentionable lusts and unspeakable cruelties (see Rom. 1:22–32) until the world was transformed.

William and Catherine Booth, the founders of The Salvation Army, shone and burned their way through immeasurable obstacles of vice, ignorance, indifference, ridicule, contempt, and stubborn opposition.

And multitudes of lesser men and women have won their way and triumphed by the same burning. I know a Salvation Army officer who burns his way to victory in every corps (church) he commands. He is an ordinary-looking man, with slender gifts, but he has the fire. He burns.

What is this fire? It is love. It is faith. It is hope. It is passion, purpose, and determination. It is utter devotion. It is a divine discontent with formality, ceremonialism, lukewarmness, indifference, sham, noise, parade, and spiritual death. It is singleness of eye and a consecration unto death. It is God the Holy Spirit burning in and through a humble, holy, faithful heart. It is the spirit that inspired young Queen Esther to go to the king and plead for her people, saying, "If I perish, I perish" (Est. 4:16 KJV).

It is the spirit that inspired Jonathan and his armor-bearer to go up singlehanded against the mocking Philistines and rout their army. It is that which inspired David to run out to meet the insolent giant and put to flight the proud foe. It is the spirit that emboldened Daniel to face the lions' den and his three friends the sevenfold-heated furnace rather than be false to God and conscience and the old-time religion of their fathers. It is the spirit that led Peter and his friends to defy the threatening rulers and go to prison and glory in whippings and sufferings for Jesus' sake. It is the spirit that led Paul and Silas to boldly preach Christ to unruly mobs and religious bigots, to rejoice in stonings and stripes, and to sing psalms in a noisome midnight dungeon until the jailer himself became a follower of Christ. It even led them to work until saints were found in the household of that half-demon Caesar Nero—he who murdered his own mother and stamped his wife and unborn child to death. He set Rome ablaze and fiddled while the city burned, then charged the Christians with the burning and had them covered with pitch and set on fire, lighting the parks and streets with flaming saints, even possibly those of his own household!

It is the spirit that inspired John Knox to cry out to God, "Give me Scotland or I die," and that led Luther—in the face of almost certain death—to say to his friends, "I will go to Worms, though there be as many devils in the city as there are tiles on the roofs of the houses."

This burning is the spirit that led young men and women of a Salvation Army corps to come to the officers repeatedly and ask for the keys to the hall so they might spend half the night in prayer, until their corps blazed with revival and growth. It is the spirit that inspired an officer in a desperately hard ministry setting—in a city full of indifference and opposition—to have an all-night of prayer every week with two or three kindred souls who shared his burden, until God moved the whole city, the mayor became his friend and protector, the city officials and pastors attended his Sunday afternoon meetings in the city hall, and the people gave him money for a new building and instruments for a big band, while the platform was filled with those who caught the flame from their leader.

How can we get the fire? Not by feasting, but by fasting. Not by playing, but by praying. Not by sleeping and slothfulness, but by watching and by diligently seeking God and the souls that wander from Him. Not by reading newspapers and devouring the comics and sporting news, but by searching the Scriptures.

Red-hot men and women are those who have become acquainted with God. They have waited for Him obediently in the way of His commandments. They have not only repented of sin and turned toward

Him, but they have also longed and watched for Him more eagerly than shipwrecked sailors watch for the morning. They have hungered and thirsted for Him, and they have found Him. And when they have found Him they have burst into flame. Holy fire kindles in every soul that lives with Him.

I recently visited a town where a schoolboy's cap was thrown up and lodged on an electric wire. A friendly boy climbed the pole and, reaching for the cap, was struck dead by the electric current. So fire of holiness and love flashes through one who touches God, slaying the old life, leaving a new creation in place of the old nature—new desires, new passions and tempers, new hopes and affections, new ambitions and visions. But while the man or woman becomes new, the religion is old—old as Pentecost and Calvary; old as thundering, smoking, flaming Sinai and the burning bush that Moses saw; old as Abraham and Enoch and Abel.

Red-hot men and women are people of faith. They believe God, and they burn because they believe. They "believe that God exists and that he rewards those who sincerely seek him" (Heb. 11:6 NLT), and therefore they seek Him diligently day-by-day and He rewards them by sweet assurances and intimations of His love and favor. They seek His face that they may behold His beauty and catch its reflection (see Ps. 27:4). They seek His will that they may do it (see Matt. 7:21). They listen for His voice that they may open the door of their hearts to Him and entertain Him as their Guest (see Rev. 3:20) and, hearing, follow where He leads (see John 10:3–5, 16). They seek His commandments, promises, and precepts, that they may live by every word that proceeds out of the mouth of God (see Matt. 4:4).

Red-hot men and women have seasons of solitude for secret prayer. They get alone with God as Jesus did in His all-nights of prayer, as John did in the wilderness, as Moses did on Sinai, and as Elijah did on Horeb. There, in deep meditation and fellowship with Him, they see how small and transient is the world with its prizes and pomp. They count it all as garbage compared to Christ, that they may know Him. They are people of prayer, praying in secret, and also seeking out kindred spirits to pray with them.

Red-hot men and women love God. They love His people, His house, His service. They love righteousness and holiness, and they hate sin and every evil way. They turn away their ears from that which they should not hear. They stand on guard at the gateway of eye and ear and every sense, lest sin get into their hearts through unguarded ways.

These red-hot men and women are self-sacrificing and self-denying. They do not entangle themselves with the affairs of this life any more than does the good soldier who goes forth to war. They do not mix with the people of the world except to do them good and, if possible, win them to Christ. They guard the fire in their hearts as their sole possession on earth and their passport to heaven.

Oh, let us be burning and shining lights, and then great shall be our reward, great shall be our peace and joy, good success shall surely accompany all our labors, and the Savior's words, "Well done," shall greet us as we are welcomed through the gates of pearl into heaven, our eternal home.

The Disappointed Angels 14

Angels excel in strength and are very wise, no doubt, but they do not know everything. And I have been wondering if those sweet angels who sang so joyously at Jesus' birth have not been greatly disappointed. Did they not expect the world to receive Him as King and gladly submit at once to His gentle, righteous reign of peace and goodwill? I think they probably did. But if so, how great must be their amazement and disappointment as the ages roll by and the exceeding sinfulness of sin is more and more revealed, the fierce malignity of the Devil is made more and more manifest, and the unreasonable and wicked unbelief of humanity becomes more and more apparent.

How reasonable it was for them to expect that the whole world would bow and worship before Jesus, and crown Him Lord of all! And when His gracious words fell from His pure lips, and His kindly miracles of healing the sick and feeding the hungry and raising the dead were performed, how high must have been their hopes that now His own would receive Him! And yet the more He displayed the glory of His grace, His tender sympathy, His pitying love, His divine power, the more malignant became the devils, the more hard and bitter became the hearts of men and women, the more cruel their hate, the more sullen and obstinate their unbelief, and the more determined their opposition.

Jesus' Sermon on the Mount, recorded in Matthew 5–8, if heeded and followed by everyone, would immediately solve all the moral problems that perplex society and banish all the moral ills that separate and afflict humanity. It is a simple, easily understood, perfect rule of conduct for all and, if adopted and obeyed, would at once give us a perfect moral society. If that sermon were heeded, our jails and prisons could be turned into warehouses, locks on doors and windows could be removed and the keys thrown away, bank vaults could be left open, armies could be sent back to useful labor, warships could be turned into commercial freighters, guns could be beaten into plowshares, police could throw away their weapons, and lawyers could become kindly advisors to the ignorant and bereaved in the proper settlement of affairs.

There would then be no more saloons, brothels, gambling dens, and dance halls. Slavery of any kind would cease to exist, for everyone would treat others as they would want to be treated. There would be no more stealing, murder, slander, gossip, quarreling, hate, envy, jealousy, lying, or hypocrisy, and moral wrong would vanish from the face of the earth overnight. All bewildering religious and educational systems could be simplified. All the ponderous parliaments and legislatures could be replaced by a few good, wise people. Nearly all the multitudinous laws enacted by those legislative bodies could be swept away and forgotten if everyone would resolve to humble themselves and take the Sermon on the Mount as their rule of life and conduct. Poverty and disease and ignorance would gradually—and probably very rapidly—be overcome. Love, brotherly kindness, compassion and tender goodwill, sympathy and helpfulness would fill the earth with peace, contentment, and innocent and pure joys.

Will such a time ever come? Not until people accept Jesus as Teacher, Lawgiver, Savior, and Lord. Will this ever happen? It happens every day! More men and women love, serve, honor, and own Jesus as Teacher, Savior, and Lord today than ever before.

Not all will accept Him. But He will conquer, not by some spectacular display of glory and power that will blind and overpower people, but by the sweet reasonableness of His doctrine and the infinitude of His love and patience. He will conquer by His truth and by His Spirit in the hearts of those who accept Him as Teacher, Savior, and Lord. He will conquer by His cross.

A stretcher-bearer was gathering up the wounded in battle. He passed a badly wounded enemy soldier who spat at him. A private who saw this said to the stretcher-bearer, "Leave that fellow to me. I'll soon make him spit no more, the dog!" But the stretcher-bearer replied, "No, let him alone until I come back. Then I'll get even with him!" When he returned, the wounded enemy insulted him again, but instead of knocking him on the head, the stretcher-bearer lifted him up tenderly and bore him away to the doctor's care. That is the spirit of the cross, and by that—and that alone—the world will be conquered by Christ.

His kingdom is a moral and spiritual kingdom, and is to be won and established by love, by moral and spiritual weapons, and by an appeal with only moral and spiritual motives. It is a kingdom of love and cannot be established by force or spectacular display.

I sympathize very tenderly with those whose hearts are heavy because of the slow progress of His conquest, and I understand how many, discouraged by the apparent hopelessness of winning the world by the preaching and living out of the gospel, look and long for His second advent in power and glory as the only means left for the overthrow of His enemies and the conquest of the world. But, personally, I look for no such spectacular victory.

Only through the blood of His cross will He "reconcile all things unto himself" (Col. 1:20 KJV). "This includes you who were once far away from God. You were his enemies, separated from him by your evil thoughts and actions. Yet now he has reconciled you to himself through the death of Christ in his physical body. As a result, he has brought you into his own presence, and you are holy and blameless as you stand before him without a single fault" (Col. 1:21–22 NLT).

Not otherwise will He ever win men and women to Himself. He had no other way that I can discover. He will conquer, but only by the cross. He will come in power and great glory some wondrous day, but not to change people's hearts, which can be done only by His cross. He will come to judge. He forever forswore the spectacular way when He refused to cast Himself from the pinnacle of the temple at Satan's bidding and chose the lowly, painful way of loving sacrifice.

If God interfered to prevent sin by some flaming spectacle of power and glory, this would ignore and destroy the freedom of the human will and render all human goodness an impossibility. If God forces us into goodness, we become good machines, not good people. God is too wise and too loving to do this. What, then, does God do to overcome our sin? God leaves the freedom of our will untouched. He presents to our will, at great cost to Himself, the most powerful motives, leading us to *choose* to be good. We can become good only by the exercise of our own free will. By these motives, shining everywhere on earth (but most resplendently in the incarnate Son and by His Spirit), He woos the free heart and waits in love.

Oh, what a lover is God! How He woos and how He waits. Angels and humans may be disappointed and cry out with the souls of those whom John saw in his vision on Patmos, "O Sovereign Lord, holy and true, how long before you judge the people who belong to this world and avenge our blood for what they have done to us?" (Rev. 6:10 NLT).

The weary ages may roll by in sin and sorrow, in toil and travail and agony and blood, because people will not listen and submit to Jesus, but God woos and waits in love, and wins—and will win, by the cross—such as are willing.

There in the Sermon on the Mount is God's ideal for a perfect society. No nation has yet adopted it—not even the church which, professing to be composed of those who accept Jesus as Savior and Lord, attempts to bring its members into full harmony with that blessed rule of life and conduct. And yet it is to this that nations, communities, families, and individuals must come, before the sins and sorrows and sufferings of humanity can be brought to an end and the angels' Christmas anthem of "Glory to God in the highest, and on earth peace, good will toward men" (Luke 2:14 KJV) be translated into fact.

There is God's plan. There is God's remedy for all the woes and wars and fears and bewilderments of humanity. If Jesus should come in person to teach and govern us, He would have nothing more to say than what He has said. He would have no other law to enact, no other plan to offer. He would still bid men and women to come to Him and learn to be meek and lowly in heart, to be sorry for sin, to repent, to mourn for their evil actions, to be merciful, to be hungry for righteousness, to be pure in heart, to be peacemakers, to be loving, to be forbearing, to be doing always to others as they would have others do to them, to be serving God with good will from the heart, and not to be seen of others.

Will human society ever be won to the standard set by Jesus? Listen to Isaiah: "He will not falter or lose heart until justice prevails throughout the earth" (Isa. 42:4 NLT). He has set Himself to this great task and He will prevail, but it will be only so fast as individual men and women are won to Him. Everyone who follows Jesus and becomes sanctified, and goes around with peace and love and goodwill and faith in his or her heart, becomes a light in the world and hastens the day of Jesus' triumph. Everyone who refuses to yield to Him, everyone who yields and then loses faith, everyone who lives a mixed life, adds to the gloom, delays the progress of His truth, and only hinders the coming of His triumph and prolongs the disappointment of the angels.

Let us bring to Him our best gifts as the wise men did on that first Christmas Day and reward His tender, wooing love and long patience by dedicating ourselves afresh to Him and to the great purpose for which He died on the cross, the fulfillment of which He still patiently waits and intercedes for, and which those disappointed angels must be waiting and longing for with unutterable amazement and wonder because of the slowness of men and women to believe and obey.

> Jesus shall reign where'er the sun
>
> Does His successive journeys run;
>
> His kingdom stretch from shore to shore,
>
> Till moons shall wax and wane no more.[1]

NOTE

1. Isaac Watts, "Jesus Shall Reign," 1719, public domain.

Greatly Beloved 15

It was very early—too early—in the morning, when I awoke from a sleep that was not altogether refreshing, and felt dull, restless, and depressed. But I remembered God, turned to Him, and cried for help and strength, when instantly as a voiceless whisper in my heart came the words of the angel to Daniel: "O man greatly beloved, fear not! Peace be to you; be strong, yes, be strong!" (Dan. 10:19 NKJV).

Peace—great peace—and strength, sufficient strength, abounding strength for my drooping spirit, were in those sweet, strong words. But my adversary, the Devil, was present to rob me of their riches.

Those words were spoken to Daniel, a great saint and prophet and governor of an empire. Dare I—how dare I—take them as spoken to me? Then I remembered that "no prophecy of the scripture is of any private interpretation" (2 Pet. 1:20 KJV), or "self-solving," but is for all who believe and obey. That thought helped me somewhat. For "all

Scripture is inspired by God and is useful to teach us what is true and to make us realize what is wrong in our lives. It corrects us when we are wrong and teaches us to do what is right. God uses it to prepare and equip his people to do every good work" (2 Tim. 3:16–17 NLT). And "such things were written in the Scriptures long ago to teach us. And the Scriptures give us hope and encouragement as we wait patiently for God's promises to be fulfilled" (Rom. 15:4 NLT). So I began to dare to apply the words to myself and get comfort from them.

But Daniel was called "beloved" by the angel. Now I felt I could understand how God could love Daniel, for he seems—of all historic characters—one of the most lovable and love-worthy. But was I beloved, lovable, or love-worthy? I dared not make any such claim. But then I remembered Jesus' words: "For God so loved the world that He gave His only begotten Son, that whoever believes in Him should not perish but have everlasting life" (John 3:16 NKJV), and Paul's words, "But God showed his great love for us by sending Christ to die for us while we were still sinners" (Rom. 5:8 NLT). And surely, whether lovable or unlovable, worthy or unworthy, it made no difference, for I was caught in the boundless sweep of those great assurances and promises. I, too, with Daniel, was "beloved," and I began to feel comforted as I appropriated the measureless riches of the angel's words and compared them with other Scriptures.

But Daniel was "greatly beloved." I might be loved, but was I, too, "*greatly* beloved"? That word, *greatly*, seemed too much. There was such a wealth of tenderness and condescension on the part of God in it that I hesitated before it. But then I remembered Paul's words to the Ephesians who were common folks just like me: "God is so rich in mercy, and he loved us so much, that even though we were dead because of our sins, he gave us life when he raised Christ from the dead" (Eph. 2:4–5 NLT), and I saw that God's great love extended to me—even to me—and so I was "greatly beloved"! And in the presence and embrace of such love, how could I fear? Fear and depression were cast out, and peace surged into my soul.

But the angel said to Daniel, "Be strong, yes, be strong!" (Dan. 10:19 NKJV). And I did not feel strong in that early morning hour. But I remembered that three times in a few verses in the first chapter of Joshua, God had said to Joshua, "Be strong and courageous. . . . Be strong and very courageous. . . . This is my command—be strong and courageous! Do not be afraid or discouraged. For the LORD your God is with you wherever you go" (Josh. 1:6–7, 9 NLT).

But those words were spoken to Joshua, a great warrior and general who God commissioned for special and great work. Could I draw comfort from them as though they were spoken to me? Well, I did. Faith must dare. What daring faith the Syro-Phoenician woman had (see Matt. 15:22–28). We can receive only as we believe. Doubt dams and diverts the river of God's grace; it freezes the flow of His benefits and mercies, and the soul dies of thirst and starves in the presence of plenty like the unbelieving nobleman of Samaria (see 2 Kings 7).

But Paul wrote to Timothy, "Be strong through the grace [the favor] that God gives you in Christ Jesus" (2 Tim. 2:1 NLT). But that, too, was for a specific individual, one who was called to a special work. Dare I apply it to myself? Yes, I dared.

Again, Paul wrote a general letter to the Ephesians, who were everyday, common people, just like myself, and said, "Be strong in the

Lord and in his mighty power" (Eph. 6:10 NLT). And as I considered these texts, I saw and felt that God wished, expected, and commanded me to be strong. And since His commands are always accompanied by enabling power, I felt that it was my precious, blood-bought privilege, as well as duty, to be strong in spirit, giving glory to God.

And peace and fearlessness and strength came into me as I entered with Daniel into that treasure-house of God's love—courage, peace, and strength. I just felt at home, where I could help myself to all the love and courage and peace and power I wanted. It was just as though my Lord said, "Oh man, greatly beloved, help yourself, take what you want. Let it be to you as you will."

An old friend of mine used to startle and amuse and challenge me by crying out, "All heaven is free plunder to faith." And in this early morning experience I began to feel that it was truly so. And now that I was in the treasure-house, I continued to examine, and I found Paul praying for the Ephesians that "according to the riches of [the Father's] glory he may grant [them] to be strengthened with power through his Spirit in [their] inner being, so that Christ may dwell in [their] hearts through faith" (Eph. 3:16–17 ESV). And that was just what I felt God was doing for me. I felt no longer dull and depressed but all alive toward God and others, and ready for service or suffering or sacrifice.

And then I read that this was all performed, not by some new, strange power I had not known before, but "according to the power at work within us" (Eph. 3:20 ESV)—the power that convicted me and brought me to Jesus and pardoned my sins and led me into the Holy of Holies, into the blessing of a clean heart and a life hidden with Christ in God.

What is that power? The same power that worked in Jesus when God "raised him from the dead, and set him at his own right hand in the heavenly places, far above all principality, and power, and might, and dominion, and every name that is named, not only in this world, but also in that which is to come" (Eph. 1:20–21 KJV). Matchless, exhaustless power! And this power was working in me!

Further, I read where Paul prayed for the Colossians, that they might be "strengthened with all might, according to his glorious power, unto all patience and longsuffering with joyfulness" (Col. 1:11 KJV). And I saw that this strengthening was for spiritual ends, to make me like my Lord—patient, longsuffering, and joyful (see Rom. 15:13; Neh. 8:10).

Finally, I remembered an experience when I was far away in the Mississippi Valley, a thousand miles from my home. I was weary, heartsick, homesick (as homesick as I would ever permit myself to be), exhausted, and lonely. I longed for the quiet and rest and comfort of home, the fellowship of my wife, and the arms of the children about my neck. In this state of weariness, loneliness, and temptation, I went to the Lord in prayer, somewhat in the spirit of repining and whining, and it seemed to me as though the Lord spoke to me just a bit sharply through His words to Joshua: "Have I not commanded you? Be strong and courageous" (Josh. 1:9 ESV).

It sounded in my heart like the sharp, quick command of an officer ordering a charge on the enemy. I braced up and replied, "I will. I will, Lord, be strong and courageous." Strength and courage possessed me, and I went to my meeting feeling as though I could run through a troop and leap over a wall (see Ps. 18:29), that I could chase a thousand, and that if I could find another fellow of the same mind and heart, we could put ten thousand to flight (see Deut. 32:30).

God loves us, each of us, however unworthy we may feel ourselves to be—loves us with a great and quenchless love, as the sun shines with a great warmth and splendor of light for each and every living thing, from humans to the vilest reptile and tiniest and most insignificant insect and mite. Let us receive and rejoice in His love with believing hearts.

And it is His will that we should have peace—unbroken and full—like a noble and exhaustless river; that we should be without fear that weakens and torments; and that we should be strong—strong in faith, strong in spirit, "strong in the Lord and in his mighty power" (Eph. 6:10 NLT), and strong through the glory and comfort of an indwelling God.

And yet we may miss it all by neglect. And we shall, if we do not esteem and cultivate His friendship—if we do not diligently seek His face day-by-day and believe. "Be careful then, dear brothers and sisters. Make sure that your own hearts are not evil and unbelieving, turning you away from the living God. You must warn each other every day, while it is still 'today,' so that none of you will be deceived by sin and hardened against God. . . . Remember what it says: 'Today when you hear his voice, don't harden your hearts'" (Heb. 3:12–13, 15 NLT).

To slightly adapt a well-worn verse:

> Lord, in Thy love and Thy power make me strong
> That all may know that to Thee I belong;
> When I am tempted, let this be my song,
> Victory for me, victory for me![1]

And what shall we offer in return for such great love, for such boundless benefits and tender mercies? Listen:

> I knelt in tears at the feet of Christ,
> In the hush of the twilight dim,
> And all that I was, or hoped or sought,
> Surrendered unto Him.
> Crowned, not crucified—my heart shall know
> No King but Christ, who loveth me so.[2]

NOTES

1. Herbert Booth, "Cleansing for Me," 1886, public domain.

2. Florence E. Johnson, "Crown or Crucify," in Meade MacGuire, *The Life of Victory* (Takoma Park, MD: Review and Herald Publishing Association, 1924), 4.

The Blessing Regained 16

A letter from a Salvation Army officer in another country reached me with an anguished cry for spiritual help. She told how, "definitely sanctified and led by the Holy Spirit in every detail," she "entered Army work as a girl of seventeen, full of zeal and ambition for the kingdom." But she came into contact with some people to whom she looked for spiritual counsel and help who were, to her mind, "scarcely saved." Through looking too much at the unfaithfulness of others, her own zeal lessened and she ceased to do as much as formerly. Instead of having continued victory, she has had defeat ever since.

For six years, she said, she has been struggling to carry on her work and to win souls while in an unsanctified state. What a dry, hard, unsatisfying struggle! She said she has often tried to live a holy life, but has not succeeded even for one day. She closed her letter with the cry, "Oh, if I only knew someone who has really reclaimed that blessing for which my soul yearns!"

How we long for a human touch—for a brother or sister who has passed over the sorrowful way we tread and can speak with the comfort of intimate knowledge to our hearts, one who understands and sympathizes and can help without condemning us. And such a One we find in Jesus. He took upon Himself our nature. He bore our sins. He is touched with the feeling of our infirmities. He was tempted in every way as we are, that He might meet this cry of our hearts, this deep human need of ours for a human touch, an understanding and unfailing sympathy. In Him we behold the condescension of God to the fathomless needs and bitterest cries of our smitten, broken hearts. And why does this sister need to cry, "Oh, if I only knew someone who has really reclaimed that blessing for which my soul yearns," since she can go to Him? It only shows the subtlety and obstinacy of doubt and fear, until I think I hear the Master pleading once again in tender rebuke, "O you of little faith, why did you doubt?" (Matt. 14:31 NKJV).

When people lose the experience of full salvation, they will never get it again if they spend their time in continual examination of their feelings and in vain regrets over lost emotions. The look must be forward not backward, outward not inward, and upward not downward. They must look to Jesus, not to other people, nor to the desolate heart that has lost His presence and joy. Attention must be given to the volitions, not to the emotions. Jesus said, "Anyone who chooses to do the will of God will find out whether my teaching comes from God or whether I speak on my own" (John 7:17 NIV). He did not say "feel." We must give our whole attention to willing and doing, not feeling.

Comfortable feelings will follow right willing and doing if we have faith. If we have faith—ah, there's the rub!

It is hard to get people to believe once they have lost the blessing. Yet God bends over them in infinite and everlasting love as eager and willing to restore the blessing as He was to give it at the beginning. "He restores my soul," cried the psalmist (Ps. 23:3 ESV). "I will restore to you the years that the swarming locust has eaten, the hopper, the destroyer, and the cutter. . . . You shall eat in plenty and be satisfied, and praise the name of the LORD your God, who has dealt wondrously with you. And my people shall never again be put to shame" (Joel 2:25–26 ESV).

God never denies a penitent, seeking, trusting soul. He will restore the wanderer (see Jer. 3:12, 14, 22) and do exceeding abundantly more than all that person asks or thinks (see Eph. 3:20), if he or she will seek wholeheartedly in simple faith and obedience.

The shepherd is eager to bring back the lost sheep. The faithful physician is glad to restore the patient to health, even if the illness was brought on by the patient's own carelessness or wrongdoing. The captain will spare no pains to rescue a drowning sailor, though it was through his or her own folly that the sailor was swept overboard. The loving father watches and waits long with an aching heart for the return of the prodigal child. And God is like the shepherd and physician and captain and father. God will not be mocked, and we trifle with Him at our peril. But:

> The love of God is broader
> Than the measure of man's mind:
> And the heart of the Eternal
> Is most wonderfully kind.[1]

God will surely give the blessing once more to this sister and any like her — and quickly — if they will cease to dishonor Him by doubting His love. How the Devil has been deceiving and mocking her, and how a heart of unbelief has given the Devil his opportunity!

"Oh, if I only knew someone who has really reclaimed that blessing for which my soul yearns," she wrote, as though God's Word, God's unchangeable character, God's boundless love revealed in Christ Jesus, were not sufficient ground for faith. But I quite understand this weakness and trembling and bitterness of doubt, for I have passed through it with tears of anguish, which were my meat by day and by night — and I know that the lost blessing may be found once more!

John Wesley used to say that most people lost the blessing two or three times before they learned how to keep it. Many years ago, during one of my campaigns in Sweden, a Salvation Army officer (minister) who had lost the blessing wrote me a letter in which she told me how she had attended one of my meetings hoping to get the lost blessing once more. I cannot quote her exact words, but I have never forgotten the substance of her letter. She said she sat through the meeting and listened with unutterable longing, but when the invitation was given to come and pray at the penitent form (the place at the altar for seeking forgiveness), she hesitated, shrank back, and did not come. She left the meeting with an added sense of loss and condemnation. She prayed in agony all the way home and tossed on her bed that night in prayer.

The next day she was sick in bed but spent the day praying, reading her Bible and my little book *Helps to Holiness*. The next day she was able to get up but went about her work with a great cry in her heart for the blessing, but no light came. On Sunday morning she arose with a breaking heart, wondering how she could face the services of the day. Long before the meeting started, she got alone with God and poured out her heart to Him, when suddenly the blessing streamed into her soul and she was flooded with light and love and peace. She went to the meeting and told her experience, and that morning the penitent form was crowded with seekers. She said they laughed and cried and told how they had longed for the blessing, and that day they had great victory.

Two years later I was going through Stockholm from Finland, and the commissioner (Salvation Army regional leader) spoke to me about that woman. He said that for a long time she had no power, but from that glad Sunday morning she had been a victorious soul, radiant with love and joy, winning souls everywhere, quickening dead corps (churches) into life and liberty, and turning barren wastes into veritable gardens of the Lord, until he felt that in time she would be capable of leading the largest ministry in Sweden.

In Australia, a Salvation Army officer told me that for ten years she had not had the blessing and that her soul was drying up. She was going about her duty in a mechanical way, with no joy or assurance in her heart, and she felt she never could get back the lost blessing. I assured her that God was not more willing to pour sunshine upon her than He was willing to shine in her heart once more if she would trust and obey. After some questioning I found that she had been bitterly criticizing a superior under whom she had worked some time before. I pointed out that this was a violation of the Lord's commands. I told her she must write him a letter, tell him his faults (if she thought best), and ask his forgiveness for having talked to others about him. She said she could not, for she knew just the spirit in which he would receive such a letter. But I assured her it made no difference how he received it—her duty was to write it, and without writing it she could not have God's favor. She shook her head and went away.

On Sunday morning, the last day of our stay in that city, she came to me and said, "I feel as though I have been in hell all night!" I replied, "You have not been in hell; you have only been in the vestibule of hell. But if you do not submit to God and do as I tell you—write that letter and let God have His way with you—you will be in hell someday, and maybe sooner than you think!" I felt confident that she was facing a crisis; that the Holy Spirit was making, possibly, a final appeal to her; and that her eternal destiny would be determined by her decision.

That night we had a great meeting. Thirty souls were at the penitent form. She sat halfway down the hall, a picture of despair. I went to her and urged her to settle it, and she came forward at once. I can see her still, down there on the other side of the world, a struggling, seeking soul. At last she promised God she would write that letter and peace began to nestle in her heart.

The next morning she came to me with a radiant face and said, "Oh, God has come back to my heart! He has been with me all night! I feel as though I have been in heaven!" Later she wrote several letters to me, saying that she had never known such depths of peace and sweetness of soul as the Lord had now given her. Then a heavy, unexpected trial came that taxed her faith to the utmost—but the Comforter was in her heart, and He did not fail her. Her faith held firm while the storm swept over her, and she was all the stronger for the trial.

I could easily cite many more examples of people who had lost the blessing who came seeking and finding once more in my meetings, and their letters to me have pulsed with joy as they related their experiences.

If you have lost the blessing, you may have it again. God waits to bless you if, with penitent heart and full consecration, you will now believe. Do it now, for Jesus has not changed in His love for you. His blood has not lost its efficacy. Only believe!

But you may be someone who is "blind, forgetting that they have been cleansed from their old sins" (2 Pet. 1:9 NLT). Such a case is pitiable indeed. But God can quicken a dead soul to life again. Jesus is the Resurrection and the Life, and the deadest, driest, most helpless soul who looks to Him will live and flourish and rejoice once more.

NOTE

1. Frederick W. Faber, "There's a Wideness in God's Mercy," 1854, public domain.

Hold Fast 17

In times of peril, when great ships are tossed on mountainous waves and plunged into deep and treacherous troughs of stormy seas, we must stand alert and responsive, ready for every duty we have learned in untroubled days.

This war-worn world has plunged into such a raging sea as it has never known before, and mighty nations are tossed like storm-beaten ships on its wild waves.[1] People's hearts are troubled. Their minds are perplexed. Their faith is tried in sevenfold-heated fires. Their patience is taxed to the uttermost while the accumulated wealth of the world is thrown with wild haste into the bottomless pit of war and the youth of the world is being swept away in storms of steel and torrents of blood. The eyes of courageous men and weeping women are strained and wearied, trying to peer through the darkness to discover a rift in the black clouds of war.

It is a perilous time! The old order changes, yielding place to the new. And we are sweeping into an era the character of which no one can forecast, yet which we hope will be more glorious than any former time.

But if this better time is yet to be, it must come not from a triumph of big guns, powerful navies, and conquering armies, but from the progress and triumph of the Spirit of Jesus into human hearts.

It is righteousness that exalts a nation (see Prov. 14:34) and the Spirit of Christ that promotes peace on earth and good will toward all. Ten righteous souls could have saved Sodom, but for lack of them the city was destroyed. Righteous men and women—people of justice, loving-kindness, goodwill, and purity—are more surely the bulwarks of nations than battleships and trained armies.

I honor the police officers and soldiers who maintain law and order, who uphold the rights of people to life and liberty and the lawful pursuits of happiness. But how immeasurably increased would be their task if God's ministers and heralds of the gospel were to cease saving souls and training them in truth and righteousness! Charles Spurgeon is reported to have said, "Take the Salvation Army out of London and you will have to increase its police force by seven thousand."[2]

No one is doing—or can do—a greater work for any country than saving men and women from sin and making them just and true and holy. In view of this, we must hold fast to the principles and spirit we have learned in calm and untroubled days. We serve our country and all humanity by doing so. An evil person—full of falsity, wrath, hasty speech, and uncontrolled passion and appetite—is a menace to any country, especially so at such a time as this, and we can find no higher service than that of saving people from all sin and getting them baptized with the Holy Spirit and the fire of truth and love.

We must hold fast to our faith—faith in God, faith in His care, faith in His superintending providence, and faith in His pity and love despite all contrary appearances. We must hold fast to our faith in His unalterable purpose to establish righteousness in the earth, with punishment for the guilty, correction and discipline and trial for good men and women, and in the end abundant and everlasting reward for those who diligently seek Him.

In times of trial, distress, and perplexity, faith must be fought for. A weak and flabby will and nerveless purpose will let faith slip. It is a priceless treasure that must be held fast. It was this deathless grasp of faith—or grasp of God by faith—that sustained the saints and soldiers of God in ages past. It was at a time when everything was swept away by invading armies and famine was stalking through the land, that Habakkuk cried out: "Even though the fig trees have no blossoms, and there are no grapes on the vines; even though the olive crop fails, and the fields lie empty and barren; even though the flocks die in the fields, and the cattle barns are empty, yet I will rejoice in the LORD! I will be joyful in the God of my salvation!" (Hab. 3:17–18 NLT).

He believed God. He held fast in the darkest hour when all the foundations on which people of the world build their hopes were ruthlessly swept away.

O for a faith that will not shrink

Though pressed by every foe,

That will not tremble on the brink

Of any earthly woe![3]

We must hold fast brotherly love and Christlike compassion. Christ's loving-kindness did not fail. When they spat on His face, crowned Him with thorns, scourged and bruised and ripped and mocked Him in His agony, He prayed for them and pitied them in their blind rage and spiritual darkness and ignorance. Oh, to be like Him! To fail is to disappoint Him at the point of battle where He has placed us. It is to defeat His far-reaching plans, and this we must not—we will not—do.

There is no time for hate, O wasteful friend:

Put hate away until the ages end.

Have you an ancient wound? Forget the wrong.

Out in my West, a forest loud with song

Towers high and green over a field of snow,

Over a glacier buried far below.[4]

We must hold fast to prayer and patient communion with God. During the war of the American Revolution, Bishop Francis Asbury, that wonderful and saintly Methodist, gave part of each hour of the day to prayer, and so—keeping his heart like a watered garden—was a true spiritual shepherd of the people. Our strength and comfort will come only from God through unbroken fellowship with Him. This can be maintained and nourished only by much prayer. When your heart is aching and breaking and darkness surrounds you, pray. Remember God and pray.

We must hold fast to the Bible. It throws floods of light upon our pathway and our duty in just such times as these. The Minor Prophets have furnished much food for my soul of late. No war-swept country of Europe suffers more than did the land of those ancient saints and seers of God, but through all the woe and desolation, the word of the Lord was their counselor and comfort, and they have a living message for us today.

In the Bible we discover both the judgments and the tender mercies, the goodness and the severity of God (see Rom. 11:22). There we find the great truths that will nourish our faith, fortify and sustain our souls, and rightly guide our conversation and conduct in dark and troubled days. Fed on these words of God, we walk with inner strength and assurance and are able to possess our souls in patience while the world reels through the storm into a bright and better day.

We must hold fast to our hope. In a time of great trouble and deep depression, the psalmist cried out: "Why am I discouraged? Why is my heart so sad? I will put my hope in God! I will praise him again— my Savior and my God!" (Ps. 42:11 NLT).

To the saints at Rome, in Caesar's household, to those who stood in constant danger of the martyr's death in all hideous forms, Paul wrote, "I pray that God, the source of hope, will fill you completely with joy and peace because you trust in him. Then you will overflow with confident hope through the power of the Holy Spirit" (Rom. 15:13 NLT). God will not fail, and we must hope on through storm and stress until the dawn of a perfect day.

We must hold fast to golden silence and sobriety of speech. Our speech should be gracious, thoughtful, healing, and helpful. "Be quick to listen, slow to speak, and slow to get angry," wrote James. "Human anger does not produce the righteousness God desires" (James 1:19–20 NLT).

Upright men and women cannot do other than to condemn wrong once they see it. They cannot be morally sound and condone injustice and evil. But if this condemnation is to effect righteousness, it must not be explosive but ordered and sustained. Then, like the tidal forces of nature, it is irresistible, and it works out "the righteousness God desires."

Finally, we must hold fast to our God-appointed task of winning souls to God's kingdom. That is a warfare from which there is no discharge, and if it is unfalteringly and faithfully waged, it will populate heaven with redeemed and happy souls and rob hell of its prey.

> Pour out thy love like the rush of a river,
> Wasting its waters for ever and ever,
> Through the burnt sands that reward not the giver;
> Silent or songful thou nearest the sea.
> Scatter thy life as the summer showers pouring.
> What if no bird through the pearl rain is soaring?
> What if no blossom looks upward adoring?
> Look to the life that was lavished for thee.[5]

Let us hold fast that which we have, that no one can take our crown.

NOTES

1. This meditation was written during World War I.

2. Original source unknown.

3. William H. Bathurst, "O for a Faith That Will Not Shrink," 1831, public domain.

4. Edwin Markham, "The Hidden Glacier," in *The Shoes of Happiness, and Other Poems* (Garden City, NY: Doubleday, 1922), 100.

5. Rose Terry, "Give! As the Morning That Flows Out of Heaven," in *Poems* (Boston: Ticknor and Fields, 1861), n. p.

What about My Future? 18

The question, "What about my future?" agitates many Christians' hearts and minds and is often anxiously asked. It is a question I have asked myself, and one which frequently gave me much concern, especially in times of weakness and weariness of body and depression of mind and spirit, until by prolonged and careful study of God's Word on the subject—and much meditation and prayer—faith triumphed over doubts and fears.

This question troubles us most when:

- We are weary and worn by overwork or sickness.
- We marry and children come—and sweet little mouths clamor to be fed, helpless little bodies have to be clothed, unfolding and eager little minds need to be educated, and the precious health of darling loved ones must be considered.

- Age creeps on at a fast pace. When we pick up our Bible some morning and find the words glimmering before us and running together, and no rubbing of the eyes or change of light will help us read with ease, and the physician we consult says, "You have reached the age where you must use glasses." When we can no longer bound up stairs or run uphill without breathing hard and painfully fast. When our digestion weakens and we must be careful about our diet. When our voice no longer rings with the full resonance of youth and sleep fails just a little in restoring all the springs of our body and mind. When gray hairs begin to show among the black or brown. When we want the younger crowd to count us as one of themselves but instead they stop their loud laughter and assume an air of decorous respect when we appear, in deference to our age. When we wake up to the fact that we are not young anymore, but that age is overtaking us—then this specter of the future sits down before us and demands our attention and persistently asks again and again, "What provision are you making for me?"

Now, what shall we answer to this question? Thank God, it can be answered. He Himself has answered it, and we can laugh at it and be glad and joyous and triumphant—if we will.

The first answer is close at hand and is good, though of itself it does not always fully satisfy us. It is this: There may not be any future before us. Death may be at our door, ready even now to strike us down! We may not live to see tomorrow, so why be troubled about it and fill today with the cares of tomorrow that may not be? Jesus Himself said,

"Don't worry about tomorrow, for tomorrow will bring its own worries" (Matt. 6:34 NLT).

> Why shouldst thou fill today with sorrow
> About tomorrow,
> My heart?
> One watches all with care most true;
> Doubt not that He will thee too
> Thy part.[1]

But suppose tomorrow does come with many others. What then about my future? I answer: Have faith in God. In the strongest, plainest possible language He has spoken to our fainting, fearful hearts and assured us of His unfailing care. And the only reason we do not have perfect peace regarding the future is because we do not have perfect faith in Him right now. Someone has said that if we could have foreseen the dangers attending our birth and the first years of our utterly helpless infancy we would have faced birth with far more fear than we now face death. But the Lord put it into the hearts of some to love and pity and care for us when we were helpless, crying, whining infants, and He will cause someone to love and pity and care for us in old age if we walk in His ways and keep a glad trust in Him. "Give your burdens to the LORD, and he will take care of you. He will not permit the godly to slip and fall" (Ps. 55:22 NLT). He bids us to consider the lilies, the grass, and the sparrows for whom He cares, and He assures us that He will far more surely care for us.

Who feareth hath forsaken
The heavenly Father's side;
What He hath undertaken
He surely will provide.

The very birds reprove thee
With all their happy song;
The very flowers teach thee
That fretting is a wrong.

"Cheer up," the sparrow chirpeth;
"Thy Father feedeth me;
Think how much He careth,
Oh, lonely child, for thee!"

"Fear not," the flowers whisper;
"Since thus He hath arrayed
The buttercup and daisy,
How canst thou be afraid?"[2]

The Hebrews were assured of God's care: "Be satisfied with what
you have. For God has said, 'I will never fail you. I will never abandon
you.' So we can say with confidence, 'The LORD is my helper, so I will
have no fear. What can mere people do to me?'" (Heb. 13:5–6 NLT).

If God allows me to occupy my body, will He not see that I have
food to feed it and garments to clothe it? He said He would (see Matt.
6:25–34). And shall I not stoutly trust Him and laugh at fear and be glad?
By His grace, I will. Nothing is more likely to disjoint our relationship

with God and precipitate trouble upon us than a faithless anxiety about the future and our loved ones.

The children of Israel had seen God's mighty works and unfailing faithfulness in bringing them out of Egypt through the Red Sea and the wilderness and up to Kadesh-Barnea, but they would not trust themselves in His hands to go over into Canaan! They said, "Why is the LORD taking us to this country only to have us die in battle? Our wives and our little ones will be carried off as plunder! Wouldn't it be better for us to return to Egypt?" (Num. 14:3 NLT). And this fearfulness proved their undoing, for while their children escaped, they all perished in the wilderness, except for Caleb and Joshua, who believed God. Job said, "What I always feared has happened to me, and what I dreaded has come true" (Job 3:25 NLT). And so it always does.

Two Salvationists—a husband and wife—felt called into ministry as officers. But they said, "No, we must educate our children," and refused. Then they lost their faith and left the Army. After some time, when their daughter was about fourteen years of age, beautiful as a picture, she went to The Salvation Army, surrendered her life to Jesus Christ, and wanted to join the ranks. But her parents said, "No, the Army will give you no social opportunities." Then the girl herself lost faith, and at sixteen—betrayed and soon to become a mother—was threatening to take her own life to hide her shame. They feared to obey God lest their children should lose educational and social opportunities. But in their disobedience and unbelief, their fears came upon them.

Do your present duty faithfully and joyfully. If we begin to be anxious about the future, it saps our joy, robs us of our trust in God, and blinds our eyes to those things we should now do to make our future safe. Our very anxiety about the future may help to produce conditions that will favor our fears and bring them in overwhelming power upon us.

Some years ago, two or three officers at a Salvation Army divisional headquarters became suspicious about their future in the Army, and they lost their joy and power. The miserable spiritual gangrene spread to the corps officers (pastors), and they lost their joy and gladness and sweet, simple trust in straining their poor eyes to look into the future that God had hidden from them and for which He commanded them to trust Him without an anxious thought. Since the officers had lost the joy and power, the poor, starved soldiers (church members) lost heart and interest. Subsequently, the light and glory fled from the worship gatherings, the public lost interest and ceased to come, the finances shrank, and the whole work languished, withered, and almost died. Those poor, foolish, fearful doubters could not see that their anxiety about the future was producing the conditions that would bring all their fears upon them like an avalanche. Not until others who were full of faith, joy, and the Holy Spirit rejoiced and prayed and shouted and rallied the doubting ones did the work recover from the blighting effect of their fear and unbelief.

The soul who doubts and fears and murmurs is walking right into the jaws of trouble. But for the one who keeps glad in God, rejoices, prays, and trusts in the teeth of hell, the path grows "brighter until the full light of day" (Prov. 4:18 NLT). God has pledged Himself to stand by such a person.

NOTES

1. Paul Fleming, in *The Optimist's Good Night*, comp. Florence Hobart Perin (Boston: Little, Brown, and Company, 1912), 231.

2. Mark Guy Pearce, *Christ's Cure for Care* (London: Hodder & Stoughton, 1902), 80.

Temptation 19

As the storm and whirlwind that twist the roots and toughen the fibers of an oak also help in its growth and development, so temptation is a part of our lot as moral beings in this state of probation. As occasional struggle with furious hurricanes and wild waves is a part of the sailor's discipline, and bloody battles and fierce danger are a portion of the soldier's lot, and difficult and hard lessons enter into the training of a student, so we are on trial. Our moral character is being fashioned and tested, and one of the most important factors in the formation of right character is temptation. An unchaste woman tempted Joseph, and he began the ascent to sublime heights of holy character and influence by resisting and overcoming the temptation.

Moses, doubtless, was tempted to remain in the selfish enjoyment of the luxury and learning and pomp and power of Pharaoh's court. But he resisted and overcame, "choosing rather to suffer affliction with the people of God, than to enjoy the pleasures of sin for a season; esteeming the reproach of Christ greater riches than the treasures in Egypt" (Heb. 11:25–26 KJV). And he became the world's outstanding lawgiver.

Daniel was tempted by the wine from Nebuchadnezzar's table, and peculiar strength was added to the temptation by the fact that he was a captive slave boy, far from home and in the king's palace, being trained for special duties in the king's service. But he "resolved that he would not defile himself with the king's food, or with the wine that he drank" (Dan. 1:8 ESV). And he received at last the highest honors the king could bestow.

Those temptations were part of their discipline and were turning points in those men's lives. They were God-permitted opportunities. Weak men would probably have yielded to the temptations and gone down in a night of moral blackness and ruin, but they overcame and— walking out into an eternal day of moral beauty and grandeur—became friends of God with holy characters that shine with undimmed splendor through the centuries. Temptation solicited them to evil, to sensual indulgence, to selfish pleasure, to personal safety, and to worldly glory. But they refused and chose the way of righteousness, self-denial, shame, reproach, and the cross. They feared, loved, trusted, and obeyed God, and God blessed them, walked with them, taught them, comforted them, and strengthened them until He could pile the cares, perplexities, and mountain-like responsibilities of empires upon them without them failing Him or murmuring at the burden.

And we, in turn, and according to our strength and duties, must be tempted. We cannot evade it, but—thank God—we, as they, can overcome it and rise by means of our fellowship with Jesus and holy men and women of all time. The Bible is teeming with encouragements to tempted souls.

We are assured that "the temptations in [our lives] are no different from what others experience" (1 Cor. 10:13 NLT). Others have gone this way before us triumphant, and so may we. Even while we are struggling with temptation, we may rest assured that others are fighting the same devil, battling with the same kind of trial. We are not alone. A great company of secret ones whom God knows is passing through the same fire with us, and if we are true we shall meet and know them by and by. No matter how strange and awful they may seem to us, our temptations are common to all humanity.

Y We are assured that "God is faithful. He will not allow the temptation to be more than you can stand. When you are tempted, he will show you a way out so that you can endure" (1 Cor. 10:13 NLT). God measures the full force of every trial and temptation, and will not allow it to exceed our strength, if we will promptly look to Him and seek His help. God allowed Satan to go only so far with Job (see Job 1:12; 2:6). And when we trust Him, He says to our temptations (as He does to the sea), "This far and no farther will you come" (Job 38:11 NLT).

We are assured that Jesus is able to sympathize with our weaknesses, "for he faced all of the same testings we do, yet he did not sin" (Heb. 4:15 NLT). And "since he himself has gone through suffering and testing, he is able to help us when we are being tested" (Heb. 2:18 NLT).

Again, we are told, "God blesses those who patiently endure testing and temptation. Afterward they will receive the crown of life that

God has promised to those who love him" (James 1:12 NLT), and we cannot have the crown of life under any other condition. How can the oak have the crown of life, strength, and lordly beauty, unless it withstands the storm? How can the soldier have the crown of victory if he or she gives up the battle and runs away from the fight?

What are we to do since we know we will be tried by temptation? The instruction of Jesus to His disciples was, "Keep watch and pray, so that you will not give in to temptation" (Matt. 26:41 NLT). Many temptations can be avoided by watchfulness and prayer. If we run carelessly into temptation, we may find it more difficult to get out than we supposed, and we may find ourselves ruined or subjected to lifelong sorrow, shame, weakness, suffering, and conflict as a result of our folly. If David had watched and prayed, as he should have, he would not have brought such shame and reproach to the cause of God as he did. If Peter had watched and prayed instead of sleeping while Jesus was agonizing in the garden, he probably would not have denied his Lord, nor cursed and sworn as he did.

If temptation comes upon us which we cannot escape, however much we may watch and pray, then we are to do like Roosevelt's Rough Riders in the thunder of battle: rush forward with a shout and fight to a finish. James said, "Dear brothers and sisters, when troubles of any kind come your way, consider it an opportunity for great joy. For you know that when your faith is tested, your endurance has a chance to grow" (James 1:2–3 NLT). Face each temptation as it comes. Fight it out.

It is well for us to consider that eternal life and heaven hang on the issue, and we must overcome or perish. We need not perish, for we are invited to "come boldly to the throne of our gracious God. There we will receive his mercy, and we will find grace to help us when we need it most" (Heb. 4:16 NLT). All of heaven is on our side. Our heavenly Father is pledged to give us more grace. Jesus is all compassion and pitying love. He cannot forget His forty days and nights of temptation in the wilderness and His agony in the garden, and "he knows how weak we are; he remembers we are only dust" (Ps. 103:14 NLT). He will surely give us grace to help in time of need. We are not to come timidly and fearfully, but boldly. If my child is in danger, I don't want him to be afraid to come to me for help. I want him to come promptly, boldly, even if it is due to his own fault that he is endangered. I am his father and he is my child and he has a right to come. And so God would have us come to Him with all confidence, and He will not fail us, but will with the temptation also make a way to escape, that we may be able to bear it.

When the Comforter Is Come 20

One cold, wintry day, the great, warmhearted preacher Henry Ward Beecher was walking down an almost deserted street when he found a little child crying bitterly. He picked up the child in his strong arms and folded the child on his broad breast. When the child ceased sobbing, he asked, "What is the matter, little one?"

The child replied, "Nuffin' is the matter since you comed!"

So it is with the troubled soul when the Comforter comes to abide. He dries our tears, banishes our sorrow, assures our hearts, and gives perfect peace. He is ever coming to men and women, but He finds them so preoccupied with their own affairs that He cannot abide with them. The floods of worldliness, pleasure, passion, and business so overflow them that, like Noah's dove when sent out from the ark (see Gen. 8:8–9), He can find no place to rest. But when He finds a troubled soul whose pleasures have dried up, whose passion is stilled, whose business is secondary to the needs of the spirit, and who hungers and thirsts for God, then He can find a resting place. Then He will abide.

This coming of the Comforter is a holy event, a solemn act. It must be preceded by an intelligent and sincere covenant between the soul and God. It is a marriage of the soul to the Redeemer and is not a trial marriage. No true marriage is rushed into carelessly. It is carefully considered. It is based on complete separation and consecration, the most serious pledges and vows. So, if the Comforter is to come to abide, to be with and in us evermore, we must come out and be separate for Him, consecrate ourselves fully and forever to Jesus, and covenant to be the Lord's "for better, for worse," and trust Him. The soul that is thus truly and solemnly dedicated to Him becomes His, and He will come to that soul to abide forever, to be a shield and an "exceeding great reward" (Gen. 15:1 KJV). What happens when He comes?

There is rest in the heart, and that rest is reflected in the face. Those who really have the blessing have peaceful faces. The eyes take on new brightness and luster. Notice how those who have the blessing look you straight in the eye. Their look is direct and penetrating. They seem to see right through you. I have sometimes felt, when holy people have been looking at me, as though the eyes of Jesus were turned upon me. Often such a look will convict the sinning and unsanctified person of his or her need and lead that person to cry for pardon and purity.

The evangelist Charles Finney went into a factory once, and some of the girls began to laugh. He looked at them until one or two burst into tears, and they had to stop the machinery and have a prayer meeting. A great revival followed.

There is certainty and confidence in the heart, and this is felt in the testimony. The testimony may not be very noisy, but it will have power, because there is no note of uncertainty and doubt in it. There is a ring of faith and knowledge and assurance that carries conviction to those who hear. The Comforter is behind it. The fire of His blessed presence is felt and this leads to unusual results. People take notice of what is said. They are no longer indifferent. A division takes place. Some will be glad and some will—strange to say—be mad. It was so on the day of Pentecost. A multitude believed and became followers of Jesus, but some were filled with mocking and rage.

Such testimony makes people feel the sweetness of the Spirit, the reality of sin, the possibility of righteousness, and the certainty of a coming judgment. The simplest Holy Spirit testimony has something of this power in it. Reality is in it, eternity is in it, God is in it, and so it has power.

In New Zealand, a seventeen-year-old girl got the blessing of holiness in one of my meetings. Her brother had laughed and made fun of her religion, but now she had the Comforter abiding with her to help her. Peace and love and power were in her heart, and a few days afterward, her brother came to her. "Say, Sis," he said, "I want to have a few words with you." He led her to another room and shut the door. Then, bursting into tears, he said, "I've been watching you these few days and I want to get saved. Won't you pray for me?" She was glad, and prayed with him, and he was gloriously saved. The last I heard of him he had been used in the salvation of six of the clerks in the bank where he worked. He said he was going to try to win them all for the service of God.

A great love for God and loyalty to Jesus Christ fill the heart when the Comforter comes. He glorifies Jesus and testifies of Jesus (see John 15:26; 16:14). And now, for very love of Jesus, service becomes natural and increasingly easy, and the soul is prepared for sacrifice and suffering. Love flows like a river when the Comforter comes.

But the Devil is not dead, and so there may be fierce and strange temptations at times. But just as the boat on the stormy sea could not go down with Jesus on board, so the soul cannot be defeated with the Comforter abiding within. "I pray that God, the source of hope, will fill you completely with joy and peace because you trust in him. Then you will overflow with confident hope through the power of the Holy Spirit" (Rom. 15:13 NLT).

> I know Thee, Savior, who Thou art,
> Jesus, the feeble sinner's friend;
> Nor wilt Thou with the night depart,
> But stay and love me to the end:
> Thy mercies never shall remove;
> Thy nature and Thy name is Love.[1]

NOTE

1. Charles Wesley, "Come, O Thou Traveler Unknown," 1742, public domain.

The Whisperer 21

A dear brother wrote, "There is such a need of solid work down this way, and I somehow do not seem able to rise to the demands. I do feel, however, that Jesus saves me, and I enjoy victory. But I do not seem to enjoy the blessing as I should. I am sure I strive with all my heart to live close to God, and there never was a time when I felt His presence more, but there is something in the way. Please pray for me!"

What can be the trouble? Having nothing from which to judge but that brief paragraph, I strongly suspect that the "something in the way" is a bit of subtle unbelief that leads him to hesitate to testify definitely to the blessing of holiness. The Enemy whispers, "You do not feel as you ought to feel; there is something in the way," but he does not recognize the Devil with his sly suggestions, and so instead of fighting the good fight of faith and resisting the Devil, steadfast in the faith, our brother has unwittingly agreed with the Devil that "something is in the way," and that something is a tiny root of practical unbelief, which frustrates God's grace.

Revelation 12:10 says, "The accuser of our brothers and sisters has been thrown down to earth—the one who accuses them before our God day and night" (NLT). How was he thrown down? Note the answer in verse 11:

- They "defeated him by the blood of the Lamb" (NLT)—that is, they believed, they trusted the efficacy of the precious blood;
- And "by their testimony" (NLT)—that is, honoring the blood by believing, they further honored it by daring to testify in the face of a mocking and accusing Devil that the blood cleanses from all sin (see 1 John 1:7);
- And "they did not love their lives so much that they were afraid to die" (Rev. 12:11 NLT)—that is, they made a complete, uttermost consecration of their lives to Him who shed His blood for them and were prepared to die for their testimony.

These three conditions, firmly and fully met, will lead one into the enjoyment of the blessing and, maintained, will make the blessing permanent. This is where many fail.

I had a great fight and gained a great victory at that point more than thirty years ago. Early in the morning, before most people wake up, the Devil whispered to me, "You don't feel as you did; you know you don't." And while I listened to him, I did not feel as I had; my joy was quenched. "If you had the blessing you would feel different," whispered the fiend. And all that day I was followed by that mocking, sinister Whisperer, and all day long I resisted and kept throwing myself upon the promise, "Whoever comes to me I will never cast out" (John 6:37 ESV). I read my Bible, prayed, and held fast my faith in the teeth of the Enemy, but no light came, no deliverance burst upon me. About all I could do was to stand with my back to the wall and fight. But that I did.

That night I went to a holiness meeting, and when I got there the Tempter whispered, "Don't testify to the blessing here; you know what a fight you have had all this day, and you will tell a lie if you testify to it." Finally, in a desperation of faith, I said, "I will testify to it! I have given myself wholly to the Lord. I have not consciously withdrawn myself out of His hands. I can do no more than trust Him. I can, I will, I do trust the blood to cleanse me now." So I arose and testified as straight and clear as I could to a present and full salvation and, oh, what a victory I got! The Whisperer fled. The mocking, teasing voice was hushed. And then I saw that we overcome him by the blood of the Lamb and by the word of our testimony when we are wholly the Lord's.

The Devil fights against definite testimony and stirs up vague, subtle doubts in our hearts to hush our testimony, "For with the heart one believes and is justified, and with the mouth one confesses and is saved" (Rom. 10:10 ESV). And thus is the Enemy overcome.

We should testify joyfully to the Lord that the blood cleanses. We should testify boldly, defiantly to the Devil that the blood cleanses. We should testify quietly to our own hearts that the precious blood cleanses. We should testify humbly to husband, wife, friend, and family that the blood cleanses. We should testify in private and public, in each other's homes and in large gatherings that the blood of Jesus, the Lamb slain from the foundation of the world (see Rev. 13:8), cleanses from all sin.

If we will give our Lord honor and glory by our humble but definite testimony, He will give us the witness of the Spirit and help us to understand and outwit our old Enemy and accuser, the Devil, who is the whisperer.

How to Keep Sweet 22

"Do tell me how to keep cool!" I implored of the secretary as I walked into a New York office on a recent, roasting, steaming hot day.

"I wish someone would tell me how to keep sweet!" she replied, with a pathetic look on her anxious face.

Strange to say, the Scriptures never tell us to keep sweet, but the Savior bid us, "Have the qualities of salt among yourselves," and then added what may stand for sweetness: "And live in peace with each other" (Mark 9:50 NLT). And Paul wrote, "Let your conversation be gracious and attractive" (Col. 4:6 NLT). Possibly the word *gracious* in this text stands for the sweetness so longed for by that secretary, but the saving power of salt was uppermost in Paul's mind.

Nevertheless, her longing to be kept sweet was a heavenly desire, no doubt placed in her by the Holy Spirit. And God was, and is, waiting to fulfill that desire. Unfortunately, too many are quite content to be sour, grouchy, ill-tempered, impatient, angry, hasty, and hurtful in speech and temper.

Some people seem naturally sweet-tempered. They are seldom disturbed. They abound in good health, good temper, and goodwill. But without God's help this natural sweetness will not last. Only the conscious and constant indwelling of the Holy Spirit can keep secretaries on hot days in busy offices, tired mothers with crying children in cramped rooms, and burdened executives with anxieties and vexations always sweet to the very end, always Christlike, always firm without stubbornness, always calm without indifference, always meek without weakness, always yielding without cowardice, and always cheery without levity or neglect of responsibility.

"Let the peace that comes from Christ rule in your hearts," wrote Paul (Col. 3:15 NLT). He does not seem to think it a difficult matter for peace always to pervade us. All we have to do is *let it*. It is at hand. We do not have to ascend into heaven to get sunshine; it pours itself in boundless floods all about us. All we need to do is open wide our doors and windows and let it in. So with this peace of God.

Paul wrote, "Let the word of Christ dwell in you richly, teaching and admonishing one another in all wisdom, singing psalms and hymns and spiritual songs, with thankfulness in your hearts to God" (Col. 3:16 ESV). What a cheerful verse that is! Some people turn as naturally and instantly to the Word of God for instruction, guidance, comfort, and courage as the magnetic needle turns to the pole. They find the Word in their hearts and mouths (see Deut. 30:14; Rom. 10:8). When they go, it leads them. When they sleep, it keeps them. When they awake, it talks with them (see Prov. 6:22). But this Word is not to be kept locked up in the heart. It is to bubble forth in springs of refreshment for others. It must be used to admonish, cheer, correct, and inspire others. It must not be a stagnant pool, but a flowing, sparkling stream, if it is to be kept sweet. And as it sweetens others, it will surely sweeten us.

Paul also wrote, "Let this mind be in you, which was also in Christ Jesus" (Phil. 2:5 KJV). Jesus sought nothing for Himself. He gave all. He was among His contemporaries as one who serves. He came not to be served, but to serve, and to give His life as a ransom for many (see Matt. 20:28). Where service is voluntary and glad, it sweetens all life. Where it is forced by necessity and done reluctantly, grudgingly, with inward discontent and fretting of spirit, it robs the soul of joy and becomes nothing other than slavery. All who would keep sweet must deliberately choose the lowly mind of the Master and rejoice in all they put their hand to do. Doing all work as unto the Lord, as though it were done for Him, will surely sweeten all work. And this can be done. It is the very ideal of the Bible. We are not to work and serve as people-pleasers but "as bondservants of Christ, doing the will of God from the heart, rendering service with a good will as to the Lord and not to man" (Eph. 6:6–7 ESV).

"Let your speech always be gracious, seasoned with salt" (Col. 4:6 ESV). No one can keep sweet who gives way to unloving speech, to fretful, complaining talk, to angry words, or to idle, critical gossip. As James wrote, "And so blessing and cursing come pouring out of the same mouth. Surely, my brothers and sisters, this is not right! Does a spring of water bubble out with both fresh water and bitter water?" (James 3:10–11 NLT). Opening the mouth in speech is like opening the draft of your fire. Shut off the draft and the fire dies down. So shut off evil speech if you would keep sweet.

Finally, "Let brotherly love continue" (Heb. 13:1 ESV). The love of God is the great sweetener of all life. The heart that loves unfailingly will be a fountain of sweet waters from which healing streams will flow. Such a heart blesses its possessor and all who are around. It is both a fountain and a fire. If the fires of love are fed with fresh fuel every day from God's Word, if they are blown upon by the breath of prayer and praise, if the drafts are kept open by testimony and service to others, they will never go out but will burn on and on until they are caught up and commingled with the eternal fires of love that burn in the hearts of and enlighten forever the angelic hosts of heaven and the very heart of God Himself. Oh, how they love in heaven! Let us emulate them upon earth, and I am sure we shall know the secret of keeping sweet. The only good thing in life is love, and every drop of sweetness comes from this.

My heart was restless, weary, sad, and sore,
And longed and listened for some heaven-sent token:
And, like a child that knows not why it cried,
'Mid God's full promises it moaned, "Unsatisfied!"
Yet there it stands. O love surpassing thought,
So bright, so grand, so clear, so true, so glorious;
Love infinite, love tender, love unsought,
Love changeless, love rejoicing, love victorious!
And this great love for us in boundless store:
God's everlasting love! What would we more?[1]

NOTE

1. Frances Ridley Havergal, "Everlasting Love," in *Compensation and Other Devotional Poems* (New York: Anson D. F. Randolph & Company, 1881), 97.

When the Word of God Comes 23

Human beings cannot by searching find out God, but God can and does reveal Himself to them. In spite of the doubts and denials of agnostics and skeptics, God can and does make Himself known to His creatures. He does communicate with them. He opens their ears. He speaks to their hearts. He tells them His secrets. He shows them things to come. He reveals to them His will.

"Now the word of the LORD came to Jonah" (Jon. 1:1 ESV). Happy man! Men and women of force and spirit like to be brought into confidential relations with their rulers, to be entrusted with responsibility and sent on high missions. And here is an unknown, undistinguished soul singled out from the crowd by the Lord God Almighty and made an ambassador of heaven. What dignity and honor!

Mighty transformations are wrought by the coming of the word of the Lord to human hearts! They can never be the same as before. It will either exalt them to the place of partners and coworkers with God and give them a seat with Jesus on His throne, or it will banish them from His presence and doom them to hell. If obedient to the word, they will be saved, empowered, and brought into closest fellowship with God, into confidential relations with Him, and they will be transformed into the likeness of His Son. But if disobedient, they will shrivel as Judas did, and in the end be lost.

It is an awesome thing for the word of the Lord to come to a man or woman. It means that person's hour has come. It means facing the opportunity and purpose for which we were born. Our destiny for eternity turns on the way we receive that word and the use we make of it.

"A still small voice" (1 Kings 19:12 KJV) speaks out of the silence of eternity into our heart, and we know that it is the word of the Lord that has come to us. And from that hour, if we hush and listen and humble ourselves to obey this voice, we will cease to be of the common herd and become heirs of God and workers with Him.

The word of the Lord came to Noah, and he hearkened and stepped out from the ranks of the men of his generation, built the ark, and became the heir of the world. The word of the Lord came to Abraham, and he believed and obeyed, left his kindred and fatherland, and went forth, not knowing where he was going. He became "the father of the faithful," and in him all the families of the earth are blessed. The word of the Lord came to Moses while he was feeding sheep on the wild, barren mountains, and he went forth with his shepherd's rod to humble Pharaoh, deliver Israel, and become the world's lawgiver.

The word of the Lord came to Saul of Tarsus, the bigoted and murderous persecutor. And, humbling himself as a little child, he became the herald of the cross to all, the flaming evangelist, the worldwide, tireless missionary, the profound, tender teacher, the masterly organizer, the love slave of Jesus, and the triumphant martyr, the apostle Paul. The word of the Lord came to Luther, one of the numberless unknown monks, and he arose a free man. And with stroke upon stroke he broke the shackles of superstition and ecclesiastical tyranny until nations were set free. The word of the Lord came to John Wesley, and he heard and went forth to nearly threescore years and ten of tireless toil. His patient, loving, unwavering, self-sacrificing service set the world on fire with love, as it had not been since the days of Peter and Paul, and turned back the tide of infidelity and heathenism that was rolling over and swallowing up Christendom.

The word of the Lord came to William Booth when he was a boy of fifteen, and The Salvation Army—with its thousands of workers in dens and pubs and slums, in the bustling city and the dreary wilderness, under the midnight sun of Norway and the tropical sun of India and Sri Lanka, in London and Paris, in Berlin and New York, and in the far reaches of Africa and Alaska—was born. The word of the Lord came to multiplied thousands of humble, unknown men and women in kitchens and laundries, in mills and mines and markets, in stores and factories and offices, on shipboard and on farms, and made them mighty in simple faith and burning love and Christlike unselfishness to confound the wisdom and cast down the strength of this world, and to establish the kingdom of heaven on earth.

The word of the Lord comes not with thunder crashes that startle the world, but in still whispers to the heart of the one to whom it is addressed. The world hears no sound, but soon knows to whom God has spoken—knows by the love-lit eye, the shining face, the elastic step, the ringing voice, the positive, courageous message, the humble, patient devotion to duty, if the word is gladly received. Or it knows by the darkening countenance, the downcast, averted, or defiant eye, and the shrinking form that drops back to the rear seats or flees to far and dark corners if the word of the Lord is not gladly received. When the word of the Lord comes to a person, it means honor and dignity and joy. But it also may mean sorrow and trial and long and sore discipline, which, if willingly embraced, will mean final and eternal and inexpressible honor, dignity, and joy.

It must have thrilled Elijah's heart with joy when the Lord came to him. But how his faith must have been tried as the Devil whispered to him each day and night, "What if the ravens do not come?" And when the brook from which he drank began to dry up; and when he— a strong man—was made dependent upon a poor, desolate widow; and when her only child died and he was reproached for its death, it must have been a fierce trial of faith, a sore discipline of patience and hope! Yet, after Elijah's struggle and long warfare, the heavenly chariot swung so low that he stepped in and was swept to heaven in a whirlwind of fire without tasting death.

It is a joyous thing to hear God's word, and through it to become a man or woman with a mission, even though to flesh and blood it proves a grievous thing. It is the only way to true peace and highest usefulness here, and to endless glory and unfailing joy hereafter. It means toil and labor and conflict, but if our faith does not fail, it means final and eternal victory, too. Paul cried out—after his sore trials, his stupendous labors, his multitudinous conflicts and sorrows, and in sight of the executioner's ax—"I have fought a good fight, I have finished my course, I have kept the faith: henceforth there is laid up for me a crown of righteousness, which the Lord, the righteous judge, shall give me at that day" (2 Tim. 4:7–8 KJV).

Jesus still asks us, "Can you drink the cup I drink or be baptized with the baptism I am baptized with?" (Mark 10:38 NIV). For it is through that gateway of trial and suffering that we enter into the realms of blessedness, from which we shall go out no more, but will reign with Him forever. "If we suffer, we shall also reign with him" (2 Tim. 2:12 KJV). "We share in his sufferings in order that we may also share in his glory" (Rom. 8:17 NIV).

It is ever by the word of the Lord that God reveals Himself to His people. Happy will you be if you have an ear to hear, a heart to understand, and the will to obey the word of the Lord which comes to you and bids you rise and be a soul-winner. You, too, may know God's secret.

The Unpardonable Sin ▌24▐ ◀

A woman who was a complete stranger to me came to me in great distress, thinking that she had committed the unpardonable sin. She had, under stress of great temptation, broken a vow to the Lord. Later, with many tears and deep penitence, she confessed to Him and believed that He had forgiven her, but felt that the Holy Spirit had left her. She thought she knew the moment when He left and, with much detail, told me all the mental and spiritual exercises and agonies through which she had passed. Fortunately, I had had a similar experience many years before, in which I thought I was lost, and for weeks I walked in an agony of mental and spiritual suffering that is hard, if not impossible, to describe. Then one morning, in the twinkling of an eye, God lifted me out of that pit as a brother read these words to me: "No thoughts which cause us disquiet and agitation come from God who is Prince of Peace; they are, rather, temptations of the Enemy [or from self-love or from the good opinion we hold ourselves], and therefore we must reject them and take no notice of them."[1]

With lightning-like rapidity my mind took in the significance of those words and I was free. I saw that I had no good opinion of myself. All self-conceit had been burned out of me by the revelation of my corrupt heart and of my utter dependence upon Another for salvation and holiness of heart. I had no self-love, but rather self-loathing, for I saw how hateful had been the pride and sin of my heart. Then I saw that these disquieting thoughts were not from God, for He is the Prince of Peace. Therefore, they must be of the Devil, and instantly it was as though an octopus loosened its long arms from about my mind and fled away. My soul nestled down into the arms of the Prince of Peace and peace—an ocean of peace—washed over my tired mind and heart and bore me up on its broad bosom, and since then peace has been the heritage of my faith.

What was my trouble? What was the trouble with the woman who came to me for advice? Just this: We were in such spiritual confusion that we had taken our eyes off Jesus.

The Son is the Mediator. It is His blood that atones for sin. He is our surety. It is in His name that we must ask for pardon and purity and power and every grace and gift. It is as though a banker gave us his bankbook and said, "Draw on me for all that you need."

The office of the Holy Spirit is to illuminate mind and heart, and to make us see and feel the great love of the Father in the gift of His Son—and the love of the Son in giving His life for us: "The Spirit . . . will testify all about me" (John 15:26 NLT); "He will bring me glory by telling you whatever he receives from me" (John 16:14 NLT);

"When the Spirit of truth comes, he will guide you into all truth. He will not speak on his own but will tell you what he has heard" (John 16:13 NLT).

The Holy Spirit is like a great searchlight, which throws its rays in a flood upon some noble object. We are not to focus upon the blinding light, but upon the object revealed by the light. So we are not to turn our eyes upon the Spirit, but on the Son, upon whom the Spirit pours His glorious light. "We do this by keeping our eyes on Jesus, the champion who initiates and perfects our faith" (Heb. 12:2 NLT). We must not turn our eyes from Jesus. He is our hope. He is the Rock of ages, cleft for us.

The Spirit also throws His light upon the Scriptures, and in them—under that glorious illumination—we find that which we are to believe concerning God and His love for us revealed in the Son. The Scriptures are the food of faith. I have never yet talked with one who thought he or she had committed the unpardonable sin—and I have talked with many—who was not continually telling me of feelings. They were starving and destroying faith by dependence upon feelings instead of nurturing it on the assurance and promises of God's Word.

They say, "I felt the Spirit leave me." The Word says, "I will never fail you. I will never abandon you" (Heb. 13:5 NLT).

They say, "I feel God has forgotten me." The Word says, "Never! Can a mother forget her nursing child? Can she feel no love for the child she has borne? But even if that were possible, I would not forget you! See, I have written your name on the palms of my hands" (Isa. 49:15–16 NLT).

They say, "I feel God has cast me off forever." The Word says, "I have chosen you and will not throw you away" (Isa. 41:9 NLT).

They say, "I feel God will not answer me." The Word says, "Call to me and I will answer you" (Jer. 33:3 ESV) and, "The same Lord . . . gives generously to all who call on him. For 'Everyone who calls on the name of the LORD will be saved'" (Rom. 10:12–13 NLT).

They say, "But I feel if I come to Him, He will not receive me." The Word says, "Come to me . . . and I will give you rest" (Matt. 11:28 NLT) and, "Whoever comes to me I will never drive away" (John 6:37 NIV). They continually examine the pulse of their feelings instead of committing themselves into the care of the Great Physician and letting Him handle their case. They look at some past failure by day and night instead of looking to Jesus, who waits to save. They weep and cry for mercy, but they won't take it when it is extended to them. They cast away hope, while He whispers, "Hope in God" (Ps. 43:5 NLT), "for God chose to save us through our Lord Jesus Christ, not to pour out his anger on us. Christ died for us so that, whether we are dead or alive when he returns, we can live with him forever" (1 Thess. 5:9–10 NLT). They continually say, "I felt," "I feel," while He says, "Believe" — "Believe in the Lord Jesus and you will be saved" (Acts 16:31 NLT). They want salvation by feeling before they take it by faith. They have lost sight of the Father and the Son and are seeking deliverance where it can never be found.

Such people feel or imagine that they have committed the unpardonable sin—the sin against the Holy Spirit—but they have done no such thing. The sin they are committing is the sin of unbelief, because they do not believe in Jesus; they turn their eyes away from Him and seek salvation in some other name. And "there is salvation in no one else! God has given no other name under heaven by which we must be saved" (Acts 4:12 NLT)—not even the name of the blessed Holy Spirit.

All the people I have ever met who thought they had committed the unpardonable sin were full of contrition. They wept and prayed and condemned themselves, and had love for the Savior, only they refused to believe that His mercies were still offered to them.

The vast ocean of His love had become a burning desert to them. It had dried up. His compassions had clean failed forever. But it was not so with those men of whom Jesus spoke when He mentioned the unpardonable sin (see Matt. 12:32). They were not anxious. They shed no tears. No fears that they had committed an unpardonable sin filled their breasts. They refused to believe the credentials of Jesus, the mighty signs and wonders He worked, the wondrous creative and recreative miracles He performed—such as opening eyes that had been blind from birth, healing lepers with a word, raising the dead, stilling stormy seas by His command, and multiplying a little boy's lunch of loaves and fishes until they fed thousands.

I say they refused to believe these acts He performed in love before their eyes to enable them to believe, to justify them in believing that He, a humble carpenter from Nazareth, was indeed the Son of God. To believe His mighty claim to be the Son of God meant that they must humble themselves, confess their sins, put away their evil actions, sacrifice their pride, and follow Him; and this they would not do. They hardened their hearts and declared that the miracles He worked in the power of the Spirit were performed not by the Holy Spirit but by Beelzebub, the prince of devils.

This was the sin against the Holy Spirit, and the reason it was unpardonable was because it hardened the heart against those evidences and gifts and tender graces which alone could produce repentance and faith, and without which there can be no pardon. I have never seen anyone whom I could truly say had committed such a sin. And I have always been able to say to those weeping, anxious, penitent souls who mourned because they thought they had sinned the unpardonable sin, that I was fully convinced that they had not committed it. I could say this with the deepest conviction and the fullest confidence.

Those who had committed that sin had no sorrow, shed no tears, felt no anxious fear. They and their kind planned the destruction of Jesus, and not only of Jesus but also of Lazarus, whom He had raised from the dead, because the raising of Lazarus led simple, honest souls to believe on Jesus. They hired false witnesses to testify against Jesus, and when Pilate would have let Him go they appealed to Pilate's fears of his master, the emperor of Rome, and said, "If you release this man, you are no 'friend of Caesar'" (John 19:12 NLT). They cried out, "Crucify him! Crucify him! . . . Kill him, and release Barabbas to us!" (Luke 23:18, 21 NLT). And Barabbas was a murderer.

And when the Roman soldiers had crucified Jesus, they "shouted abuse, shaking their heads in mockery. . . . The leading priests, the teachers of religious law, and the elders also mocked Jesus. 'He saved others,' they scoffed, 'but he can't save himself!'" (Matt. 27:39, 41–42 NLT). So He meekly bowed His head and died, while they mocked and refused to believe. There was sin, ripe and full and unpardonable, because it had carried those who were committing it beyond the power of tears and penitence and sorrow for sin. And such is the sin against the Holy Spirit, which "will never be forgiven, either in this world or in the world to come" (Matt. 12:32 NLT).

No one whose heart is broken with sorrow for his or her sins, and who is willing to come to Jesus and trust His atoning love, has committed that sin or any sin that is its equivalent.

Look to Jesus. Turn your eyes from yourself, your feelings, and your failures, and fix them on Jesus. Behold the Holy Spirit pointing you to Jesus, and hear the Spirit whispering, "Behold, the Lamb of God, who takes away the sin of the world" (John 1:29 ESV).

Look to Jesus. He is our hope. He is our peace, and if you believe in Him you shall "not perish but have eternal life. God sent his Son into the world not to judge the world, but to save the world through him" (John 3:16–17 NLT).

NOTE

1. St. Francis de Sales, *Letters of Spiritual Direction*, trans. Péronne Marie Thibert (New York: Paulist Press, 1988), 120.

Speaking with Tongues and the Everlasting Sign 25

When God sent Moses to free His people from Egyptian bondage and usher in the dispensation of the law at Sinai, He confirmed the message of His servant with signs and plagues and a great deliverance. And so, when the new dispensation of His Son was inaugurated, we read that "God confirmed the message by giving signs and wonders and various miracles and gifts of the Holy Spirit whenever he chose" (Heb. 2:4 NLT).

Among these signs and gifts of the Holy Spirit was "the ability to speak in unknown languages" (1 Cor. 12:10 NLT), mentioned in the Acts of the apostles and in Paul's first letter to the Corinthians. The bare mention of this gift is found in Acts, but in the church at Corinth it seems to have been one of a number of burning questions that required Paul's attention. And so, besides mentioning it in one chapter, he devoted another long chapter to a discussion of its relative value and its regulation.

The Corinthian church, while apparently vigorous and gifted, was not spiritually healthy. There were contentions among them (see 1 Cor. 1:11), arising from their divided preference for certain leaders (see 1 Cor. 1:12; 3:1–7). In at least one instance, there was practiced the most shameful licentiousness (see 1 Cor. 5:1–13). They went to court against each other before unbelievers (see 1 Cor. 6:1–8) and were unsound in their views of marriage (see 1 Cor. 7). Some of the men were gluttonous and others drunken (see 1 Cor. 11:21), while others of them seem to have been afflicted with conceit and spiritual pride (see 1 Cor. 14:36–37).

Paul fairly confronted all these conditions and wrote a letter full of homely, practical, and spiritual instruction to enlighten their understanding and correct their glaring faults.

In chapter 12, he mentioned nine gifts of the Spirit, seven of which were mentioned before "the ability to speak in unknown languages" (1 Cor. 12:10 NLT). And yet these Corinthians attached so much importance to the gift of tongues that Paul devoted one of the longest passages to showing how comparatively unimportant it is and how much better it would be for them to seek other gifts that were far more useful. Indeed, he said, "As for tongues, they will cease" (1 Cor. 13:8 ESV).

From a study of chapter 14, we learn:

1. That those who speak in unknown tongues speak not to other humans but to God (see 1 Cor. 14:2), and that they should not speak in church but keep silent, unless someone interprets (see 1 Cor. 14:28).

2. That while speaking in an unknown tongue may edify the one who speaks, it does not edify those who hear (see 1 Cor. 14:4), and it

leaves the speaker's own understanding untouched, by which it would seem to be a sort of ecstasy which can do no permanent good.

✗ 3. That instead of making sounds which are unintelligible both to ourselves and others, we should most earnestly desire to sing, pray, and speak with the understanding (see 1 Cor. 14:9, 15, 19). The apostle is here, as always, intensely practical and full of common sense, for he exalted that which is useful above that which is spectacular and exhorts the Corinthians to seek the gift of prophecy which will intelligently bless people, rather than the gift of tongues which may make them stare and wonder and go away unblessed, as he hinted that their preference for tongues was an evidence of childishness and infantile understanding, which prefers the gaudy toy to that which is highly useful (see 1 Cor. 14:20).

✗ 4. That Paul considered prophecy to be more valuable than speaking in unknown tongues (see 1 Cor. 14:19). Prophecy here does not mean foretelling future events but "forthtelling," out of corresponding experience, the saving and glorious truth of the gospel of Christ in a message that will edify, correct, and comfort (see 1 Cor. 14:3).

✗ 5. That the gift of tongues is not a sign to believers that they have the Holy Spirit but to unbelievers (see 1 Cor. 14:22), and it will be no sign to them if there is no interpreter. On the contrary, they will consider the speaker to be insane (see 1 Cor. 14:23).

✗ 6. That speaking in an unknown tongue hinders united worship and communion of spirit (see 1 Cor. 14:16–17). For people cannot say "amen" to what they do not understand, nor be blessed by a babble of meaningless sounds. Indeed, it may even do harm and work damage by leading the hearers to mock at what to them seems like the cackle of hysteria or the ravings of them that are insane (see 1 Cor. 14:23).

7. Finally, that the apostle did not become vexed and impatient with those who in ecstasy of joy or devotion and spiritual rapture speak an unintelligible language. "Don't forbid speaking in tongues," he wrote (1 Cor. 14:39 NLT). But we must not forget that he forbade them to speak in public unless there was an interpreter.

Paul's heart was full of the love of which he wrote in chapter 13, and he wanted that love to abound in the Corinthians' hearts. Love will make those who do not speak in tongues patient with those who do, so that they will not forbid them to speak. And love will make those who speak in tongues exercise their gifts in private before the Lord, for their own edification, instead of in public when there is no interpreter, to avoid offense and confusion.

In case there were any who thought that by keeping silent they grieved the Holy Spirit, Paul added, "People who prophesy are in control of their spirit and can take turns. For God is not a God of disorder but of peace, as in all the meetings of God's holy people" (1 Cor. 14:32–33 NLT).

As a wise and devout commentator has written, "This means, not that the divine Spirit should be overruled, but that the disorder of the human spirit, under divine influence, should be steadied and ruled by the rational faculty, in accord with the principles of order and becomingness."[1]

So here let none claim that they are obliged by the powerful and uncontrollable impulses of the Spirit to overbear reason, order, or decency. And that such claims of being moved by the divine Spirit to disorder are false is clear from the solemn fact that "God is not a God of disorder" (1 Cor. 14:33 NLT).

Where confusion or disorder occur, it is due to the uncontrolled human spirit and is a violation of God's will as expressed in His Word.

As floods of water flowing into a canal can accomplish a useful purpose only so long as the banks are sufficiently high and unbroken to hold the water, so the Holy Spirit coming into a person can only fulfill His gracious purposes so long as that person's spirit is firm and under strong and intelligent discipline and control. And it is for the guidance of such discipline and control that the apostle wrote this long passage on the gifts of prophecy and tongues.

These gifts, the apostle assures us, shall not continue. "As for prophecies, they will pass away; as for tongues, they will cease" (1 Cor. 13:8 ESV). In the minds of many, the special significance of this chapter is a thing of the past, and it is without application to us today. But this is not true. The gift of tongues may or may not have ceased, but the great principles of the chapter abide for our guidance. And we are only safe from the delusions of the Devil and of our own spirits as we carefully follow its plain principles and instructions. Running through it all is the heavenly love that seeks to edify rather than to amaze and mystify, which knits hearts together in divine unity and fellowship instead of driving them asunder by disorder and confusion.

NOTE

1. Daniel Denison Whedon, *Commentary on the New Testament, Intended for Popular Use*, vol. 4 (New York: Phillips & Hunt, 1875), 110.

The Fleeing Prophet 26

Men and women who do things for God and who have God on their side usually, in the beginning, find their way rough, hedged in, and difficult. "It is good for people to submit at an early age to the yoke of his discipline," wrote Jeremiah (Lam. 3:27 NLT), and this is their lot and their portion. Their hearts are encouraged and their spirits supported not by favorable circumstances and applauding crowds and smiling heavens, but by a stern sense of duty; a secret, silent whisper of faith and hope; and a hidden fire of love which "laughs at impossibilities and cries: 'It shall be done!'"[1] With Queen Esther they say, "If I perish, I perish" (Est. 4:16 KJV), and follow where God leads. With Job, they say, "Though he slay me, yet will I trust in him" (Job 13:15 KJV).

It was doubtless so with Noah through those long years of waiting and working, while the faith was being fashioned and tried which made him heir of the world. It certainly was so with Joseph, through those years of slavery and imprisonment before he was lifted up to Pharaoh's side and made ruler of Egypt and set to teach his senators wisdom. It was so with Moses during those forty years in Pharaoh's palace as the reputed son of Pharaoh's daughter, in which he mastered the wisdom and learning of Egypt, and those other forty years when his masterful spirit was chastened among the mountains and in the desert, feeding sheep. It was so with David and Daniel and Paul. It was so with William Booth. They struggled on against ridicule, reproach, and persecution, when to human vision it seemed that God Himself, if not against them, was indifferent to them. They were possessed of the spirit of John Milton, who—poor, old, and blind—wrote:

> I argue not
> Against heaven's hand or will, nor bate a jot
> Of heart or hope; but still bear up and steer
> Right onward.[2]

They knew the secret of the psalmist, who wrote: "You have tested us, O God; you have purified us like silver. You captured us in your net and laid the burden of slavery on our backs. Then you put a leader over us. We went through fire and flood, but you brought us to a place of great abundance" (Ps. 66:10–12 NLT). In due time, when He had tried and proved them, the universe saw that God was on their side.

They did not consult with their convenience or their fears, but only with their sense of duty and their heart of faith and love. Thus they were unmoved amid the storm and trial, and prospered. They did not observe the winds before sowing, nor regard the clouds before reaping.

In the morning they sowed and in the evening withheld not their hand (see Eccl. 11:6). Like Joseph, they would not commit sin to escape persecution. Nor would they turn aside a hair's breadth from the path they had marked out for themselves to avoid chains and dungeons. Nor would they shut themselves up in some quiet temple to save their lives. They did not judge the righteousness of their cause by outward appearance, nor compute the possibilities of success by favoring circumstances and applauding multitudes. They were kindred spirits to the one who

> Through the heat of conflict, keeps the law
> In calmness made, and sees what he foresaw.[3]

But how different are men or women who are running away from duty and God! Circumstances seem to favor them. The south wind blows softly and, in spite of the warnings of wisdom and goodwill, they sail away to storm-swept seas to wreck and ruin.

We read of Jonah, "He found a ship" (Jon. 1:3 NLT). "How lucky!" he must have thought. "What good fortune! My stars favor me! So far all is well!"

Oh, the wayward souls who find ships waiting for them and, forgetting God, duty, faith, and the souls who lean upon them, take counsel with their seeming good fortune, hug themselves with complacency, and blithely set sail for Tarshish!

Absalom found Ahithophel and the men of Israel ready to flock to his standard when he raised it in revolt against King David, his father. He "found a ship." Judas found the high priest and his party ready to pay hard, cold cash for the betrayal of Jesus. He "found a ship." These are terrible examples. But we often find men and women illustrating in their lives the same principle.

A Salvation Army officer (pastor) left his post, reviled his former leaders and old colleagues, and found a rich man ready to provide him a home and job with a big salary, which he at once accepted. "He found a ship." Another ran away from his post and at the first place he visited, he found that they wanted a cook, and since he was a cook, he felt highly favored and was delighted. "He found a ship." But storms soon overtook both of those ships, and most interesting and instructive was the sequel.

Run away from the duty to which God in infinite wisdom and fore-knowledge calls you, the path which He in boundless love marks out for you, and the Devil will surely arrange to have a ship ready to carry you down to Tarshish. But he cannot ensure you against a storm, and he would not if he could. Storms certainly await you, however softly the south wind may blow.

You remember what happened to Jonah. You know the end of Absalom and Judas. Not that I would for an instant compare you with them, but the smallest disobedience is a step toward the steep and awful decline that leads to doom.

My officer friends, like multitudes of others whom I could mention, were soon overtaken by storms of unrest and disappointment and were swallowed and lay in the belly of trouble, shame, and sorrow, until the Lord in mercy delivered them and they found their way back to the port they had deserted and went, humbly and wisely, on their belated way to their appointed Nineveh.

NOTES

1. Charles Wesley, "Father of Jesus Christ, My Lord," 1742, public domain.

2. John Milton, "To the Same," lines 6–9, 1655, public domain.

3. William Wordsworth, "Character of the Happy Warrior," 1806, public domain.

Songs as Aids to Devotion

I recommend the hymns of the church—and in particular *The Salvation Army Songbook*—for devotional reading. Like the Psalms, these songs were written to be sung, and it is through singing that we get the most help and inspiration from them. But, like the Psalms, they may also be read with immeasurable blessing and profit.

They scale the heights and delve the depths of Christian experience. In them the sweetest, choicest saints and Christian warriors of many centuries and countries tell us of their struggles, hopes, fears, heart-searchings, defeats, recoveries, victories, triumphs, and divine revelations and discoveries. They will not give up their sweetness and strength to those who read carelessly and in haste; but to those who, unhasting, read with thought and prayer they open a treasure house of spiritual instruction, comfort, guidance, inspiration, and encouragement. They provide a fat feast of the best things with the finest and most gracious spirits this world has ever known.

The overworked mother or father, the common laborer, the mechanic or clerk or teenager who becomes familiar not alone with the tunes and words of a few songs but who knows them well and has grasped the experiential meaning of the songs will have become almost a master in practical and experiential theology. Such a person will be better equipped to explain the mysteries of redemption and to deal with seeking souls than nine-tenths of all the theological students graduated from seminaries and universities.

And while these songs enlighten, enrich, and enlarge the mind, they more particularly kindle devotion in the heart and make us feel the reality and pull of eternal things when they are read with thought and prayer. It is more for this that I myself read them, for it is this keen and alert sense of the things of the Spirit and of eternity that will keep our devotion alive and warm and tender.

It is this devotional spirit—the spirit of love, faith, sacrifice, and spiritual worship—that is at the same time most important and most difficult for us to maintain. Without it, we perish. "Would that you were either cold or hot!" said the Master to the church at Laodicea. "So, because you are lukewarm, and neither hot nor cold, I will spit you out of my mouth" (Rev. 3:15–16 ESV). They either lost or never had the spirit of devotion, and so a dreadful condemnation and doom awaited them. And such will await us if we become lukewarm.

But how shall we keep up this grace, this tenderness, this devotion of spirit? Never have there been so many helps, and never were there so many hindrances as now. The helps are on every hand, but the hindrances are omnipresent, too. I wake up in the morning and the patient, silent, watchful, wooing Holy Spirit is brooding over me, waiting to help me praise God and worship and pray with my waking breath. The Bible and *The Salvation Army Songbook* are there to guide my thoughts and my utterances, and when I kneel and open them, it is as though I were in a blessed prayer and praise meeting with Moses, Joshua, Samuel, Job, David, Isaiah, Daniel, Jonah, Jeremiah, Matthew, Luke, John, Paul, Peter, Martin Luther, Charles Wesley, William Booth, Emma Booth-Tucker, Isaac Watts, Reginald Heber, John Lawley, and such kindred spirits, and the fire of love ought to kindle and burn in my heart, and my soul ought to soar and shout and sing for joy.

But maybe the sun is up; business presses; the express train—like time and tide—waits for no one; and the morning paper is at the door with its welter of world news and gossip, its tales of murder and robbery, divorce and war, baseball and stock markets, diplomacy, funny and utterly foolish pictures, and—unlike the Holy Spirit and the Bible and songbook—these are noisy, loud, and insistent. It is one of the easiest things gradually to yield to and be finally overcome by them, until the heart that was once hot with love and zeal has become lukewarm and the tongue that was once a flame of fire is now a spiritual icicle. The reading of the songbook, with set purpose to drink in the spirit of the songs and to get blessed, will help one to escape this subtle and deadly temptation.

We can never more be cold toward Jesus or think mean and little thoughts of Him if we drink in and live in the spirit of these songs.

See from His head, His hands, His feet,

Sorrow and love flow mingled down!

Did e'er such love and sorrow meet,

Or thorns compose so rich a crown?

Were the whole realm of nature mine,

That were a present far too small;

Love so amazing, so divine,

Demands my soul, my life, my all.[1]

In these songs we find inbred sin and corruption—in all its subtle workings—exposed, and the way of heart purity and holiness made plain. We find Christian experience in all its phases illustrated. We see how the saints have struggled with our problems, our sins and weaknesses, our uncertainties and heart deceitfulness, our perplexities and temptations. We find that we are not traveling through an unbroken wilderness but over a highway made plain by unnumbered saints who have traveled its rough ways and full lengths and beaten them smooth on their knees. We find warnings, instructions, and encouragements all the way from the penitent form to the banks of the river and the gates of pearl.

Here we learn how others have fought sin, unbelief, and devils and overcome; how they stirred up the gift of God within them, believed and overcame in spite of hell; how they prayed and wept, shouted, sang, and fought their way through, triumphing over every foe; and how they encouraged their troubled and perplexed hearts with God's promises and past blessings and sat down at His table and fed on fat things in the very presence of their enemies. Oh, if you want to be spiritually robust and filled with holy laughter, feed your mind and heart on the songbook. Here you will get glimpses of the bitter remorse and woes of hell and be keyed up to resist sin and try to snatch souls from the yawning pit. And here you will get visions of the rest, sweetness, and sinless bliss of heaven, of the jubilant throngs of the redeemed, and of the white-robed, radiant armies of the saints who have overcome and are now crowned and bathed in light in the unveiled presence of their Lord.

Many years ago I began to read hymns just for blessing my own soul. And later, while lying helpless in the hospital, not knowing but that my end was nigh, and informed that my wife, the darling of my heart, was given up to die, I turned to the sections labeled "Heaven" and "Comfort and Guidance," where I found a whole armory of tried weapons, and with them and my Bible I fought crowded devils and thronging fears and got victory.

One day at a camp meeting I sat alone under great trees with a Salvation Army colonel (later a commissioner) who had just lost his wife. He quoted Charles Wesley's "Wrestling Jacob":

> Come, O thou Traveler unknown,
> Whom still I hold, but cannot see!
> My company before is gone,
> And I am left alone with Thee;
> With Thee all night I mean to stay
> And wrestle till the break of day.[2]

And as in deep and quiet tones he spoke the words of that noble hymn, the power and value of our songs as devotional helps (when spoken or read, apart from singing) burst upon me as never before.

Another time, I was in Australia, sitting amid the flickering lights of a slowly dying fire one night, when an old saint quaintly quoted one of our songs, one verse of which has been like a sheet anchor to my soul ever since:

> His love in time past forbids me to think
> He'll leave me at last in trouble to sink;
> Each sweet Ebenezer I have in review,
> Confirms His good pleasure to help me quite through.[3]

Let me exhort you to sing "psalms and hymns and spiritual songs among yourselves, and [make] music in your hearts" (Eph. 5:19 NLT). Keep hymns and spiritual songs by your bedside with your Bible and carry them with you on the train to read. They will enrich your faith, invigorate your hope, and keep warm and tender your love.

NOTES

1. Isaac Watts, "When I Survey the Wondrous Cross," 1707, public domain.

2 Charles Wesley, "Come, O Thou Traveler Unknown," 1742, public domain.

3. John Newton, "Begone, Unbelief," 1779, public domain.

An Accident 28

From infancy my life has been punctuated by tragic losses, surprises, and pains. I do not remember my devout father. He made the soldier's supreme sacrifice during the American Civil War when I was a little child, and my earliest recollections are of a bereaved and weeping mother, sighing, sad-faced, and heartbroken.

In my adolescence, when a young fellow most needs his mother, I was away from home at school when I received my first telegram. It read: "Come home. Come quickly. Mother is dying." When I reached home my mother, in whose heart I had lived—who had taught me to pray and had planted deep in my young heart the reverent fear of God—lay with folded hands and infinite serenity and peace on her loved face, dead. For the next twelve years, I had no home.

At the beginning of my Salvation Army ministry, a Boston rough hurled a brick at my head and felled me with a blow that laid me up for eighteen months and gave me a shock from which I have not wholly recovered in thirty-five years.

In the midst of my Army ministry, I was stricken with an agonizingly painful and dangerous sickness in a far-off land, where I lay at death's door among strangers for weary weeks, returning home at last almost helpless, a mere shadow of a man. Some years later, lying in a hospital with a great surgical wound that threatened my life, word was brought to me that my sweet wife, the darling of my life, was dying. And now at sixty-four years old, I find myself battered and broken from an automobile accident.

I do not argue, though in fact it may be so, that these are the best things that could have befallen me. But I do testify that by God's grace, by His wise and infinitely loving—if mysterious—overruling, they have all worked together for my good, for the enrichment of my soul and, I trust, of my ministry. They have worked in me to humble my proud and wayward nature. They have thrown me back on God. They have made me think. They have led me to deep searchings of heart in lonely and still hours of the night and to patient and prolonged searching of the Bible and of history to find out God's ways with humanity. They have been rigorous and unsparing but also unfailing, compelling teachers of fortitude, patience, sympathy, and understanding. They have taught me the solidarity of humanity, have revealed the brotherhood of all, and have drawn out my heart in sympathetic understanding of others. For danger, loss, and suffering draw us together and make us conscious that we are drawn up in one bundle of life together for prosperity or woe, while joys and pleasures and abundance separate people into rival groups, contending for mastery and selfish interests, forgetful and indifferent to the welfare of others. Let earthquake, famine, pestilence, fire, or flood devastate a city or a country, and how instantly the hearts of people flow together in self-forgetful, sacrificial helpfulness and sympathy!

It is worthwhile occasionally to meet with some tragic trouble just to discover this fact or to have it confirmed anew, and especially to discover what a glorious company is the secret order of the sons and daughters of God—and what instant and intimate fellowship we have in the church and The Salvation Army when some big hurt comes.

I was not yet on my proper cot, and the surgeon was still examining my injuries, when anxious brothers and sisters came to inquire about our safety. And I was hardly through breakfast the next morning when two fellow officers, who had traveled all night from Chicago, walked into my room with others, looking like angels. And angels—God's messengers of love—they were.

Another colleague, without my knowledge, had spoken for a trained nurse, and when she was not properly forthcoming, got her quickly and installed her over me with the sweetest but firmest admonition that I was to obey her and that I must at once stop talking and relax. "For," said she, "you are more deeply shocked than you imagine."

This I soon found to be true. The wild excitement of the accident, in spite of the hard blows, seemed to fling me upward on the crest of a great wave. But I soon found myself in the deep trough of a troubled sea of physical depression and pain. I shall not soon forget what a long and painful journey it was as I laboriously turned over in bed from my right side to my left and back again, and how—to relieve the strained muscles of my neck—I moved my head by pulling the hair on my forehead.

Not only did colleagues, friends, and citizens—including the mayor of the city who made three visits to me—begin to pour in, but also messages by cable, wire, and letter flooded me. And nearly everyone asked how it happened.

Well, of course, it was all "the fault of the other fellow." My colleagues and I had been conducting spiritual campaigns in the area for five weeks, and between four hundred and five hundred souls had sought pardon and purity. The presence and power of the Holy Spirit were manifest in every place. We were driving to Grand Rapids, Michigan, for our final week and were full of quiet and joyful anticipation of a time of unusual blessing.

We lunched at Muskegon and then continued in the car that had brought us from Manistee. We had forty-eight miles of finely paved road ahead of us when about four miles out in the country we found ourselves with a perfectly clear right-of-way one instant, but the next instant perfectly blocked. A reckless or unfortunate driver in a big sedan collided with the stationary car on the other side of the road, skidded across our path, and struck us broadside like the shock of doom. It was as sudden, unexpected, inescapable, and about as irresistible as a thunderbolt. Our lighter car crumpled up, turned over twice, and piled itself on top of us. The engine was on my chest, and my companion was pinned across my hips. My left elbow was pressed so deeply over my heart that I feared I would lose my breath. My right side was caved in, my shin was nearly crushed, and a blood vessel burst just below my knee, while I was bruised from head to foot. The women were lying under the wreck behind and crying feebly for help. The engine poured oil into my eye, ear, and over my uniform, until I was soaked to the skin. My stomach was dispossessed of my noon lunch and such remains of breakfast as it had not otherwise disposed of, while the clouds poured down rain.

We were soon rescued by passing automobiles. An ambulance came and took away three of our wounded and two from the other car, while I, dazed and aching, stalked around in the rain picking up mangled suitcases and wondering how I was to get to Grand Rapids.

At last a gentleman kindly suggested that it might be well for me to go back to Muskegon and be examined for injuries, and since our car was wrecked and my driver gone, I consented and was soon glad the trip to the hospital was only four miles instead of forty-four to Grand Rapids. The least jolt of the car hurt my side. Great was my surprise to hear the extent of my injuries and the time I would have to stay in the hospital. And great was my sorrow at missing my week of meetings. But I confess I felt a secret but abiding joy welling up within me that I should have been chosen as one among others to have such an awesome if painful experience. For I felt deep inward assurance that this, too, could and would be made to work for my good, for the greater glory of my Master, and possibly for the admonition and strengthening of the faith of some of my coworkers.

When I have said this to some friends they have eyed me quizzically for a moment, as though they thought my head had received a greater shock than at first suspected and that I had not fully recovered from it. They have turned their eyes away and remarked with something like a sigh, "Well, it may be so, if you can look at it in that way." But that is the only way I can look at it and get comfort and strength to bear it with patience and joy, or harmonize it with what I know of

God's character and will and ways with us, as revealed in the Bible where it shows the afflictions He permitted to fall upon His saints and soldiers of old.

Messages came in from near and far, telling of anxious fears, tender sympathy, ardent prayers, and sweet affection. And in many of these messages were such questions as, "Why this?" "Why did it befall you whose hands were so full of useful work? Why did it not fall upon someone who was doing nothing, or who had nothing to do?" "Was it devil, man, or God that precipitated this upon you?"

Such questions are natural, but are they asked in wisdom? Is there a sure, cut-and-dried answer? But all morally earnest and thoughtful persons meeting with such an accident will find in the secrets of their own hearts some answer or answers.

One will find it in some moral or spiritual need or danger, discovering that he or she had begun to drift, to neglect prayer, to become too much absorbed with the things of this life. Paul said he himself was in danger of undue exaltation through the abundance of the revelations given him; therefore God let him be humbled by Satan's thorn.

Another may find his or her answer in a new and needed line of service, in comforting and strengthening other afflicted ones, or in revealing Christ's sufficiency for suffering, as well as service or sacrifice. Sometimes we must wait patiently and watch for an answer, the very silence and uncertainty speaking to us, as Jesus to Peter, "You don't understand now what I am doing, but someday you will" (John 13:7 NLT). God may have infinitely bigger purposes than any we imagine. "I looked for a dewdrop, and found an abyss," wrote one man as he considered the infinite sweep of the plans and purposes of God.[1]

Personally, I was much comforted by the thought that "all things work together for good to them that love God" (Rom. 8:28 KJV), and that this was an opportunity to prove to myself and possibly reveal in some measure to others the all-sufficiency of His grace for suffering as well as for service. It is easy to preach in full and robust health about "grace as fathomless as the sea . . . grace, enough for me."[2] But the test comes in proving and practicing it in danger, broken health, poverty, loneliness, neglect, and sore trial.

> The toad beneath the harrow knows
> Exactly where each tooth-point goes.
> The butterfly upon the road
> Preaches contentment to that toad.[3]

The rub will come to that butterfly when it, too, gets under the harrow. Can it preach contentment then?

Truly, I would not like to go through life without some hard blows when so many of my fellow humans must suffer them, and when my Master was a "man of sorrows, and acquainted with grief" (Isa. 53:3 KJV), wounded and bruised. If I am to understand Him and my fellow humans, I must share in the common experience of life. If I am to have wide knowledge of His power and willingness to help and sustain, I must have wide experiences that call for His help. A manifold testimony with power demands a firsthand knowledge of manifold mercies. The value of testimony depends upon the degree and certainty of knowledge.

Lost? I have known that, but He found me. Guilty? Condemned? Undone? I have known that, and He forgave me. Unclean? I have known the impurity of my own heart, but He cleansed me. Weak? Powerless? I have known that, but He baptized me with the Holy Spirit, and power came into me. Poor? I have known dire poverty and have been without a dollar, but He clothed and fed me. He said He would, and He did. Lonely? I have wandered with aching heart through the dark labyrinthine dungeons of loneliness, and I found Him there and was no longer lonely. Perplexed? Bewildered? I have been at my wit's end, but He was not at His wit's end. He lightened my way.

Fearful? Afraid? I have known nights of torturing fear, and then He has drawn close and said, "It is I; be not afraid" (Matt. 14:27 KJV), then all my fears have fled away, and I wondered at the fullness of my peace and calm. Sickness? Danger? I have lain hard up against the gates of death, looking for them to open. But He has the keys of death. And He did not open, and I came back and am here instead of over there—here, singing, "My soul, be on thy guard,"[4] instead of over there singing the song of Moses and the Lamb (see Rev. 15:3) with the multitude which no one can number. Pain? Agony? I have been wracked and tortured until it seemed I could bear no more. And then I remembered His pain and agony for me on Golgotha, and my spirit bowed in adoration and rose up in exultation that I should be permitted to know something of His physical agony, and then I welcomed pain with a shout of solemn, triumphant joy. My pain seemed to fade away, and I forgot it in the fullness of my peace, joy, and fellowship with Him. God has not promised us freedom from affliction, but He has assured us that "our light affliction, which is but for a moment, is working for us" (2 Cor. 4:17 NKJV). What servants are our afflictions!

He does not make pets of His people, and especially of those whom He woos and wings into close fellowship with Himself and fits and crowns for great and higher service. His greatest servants have often been the greatest sufferers. They have gathered up in themselves and endured all the pains and woes, sorrows and agonies, fierce and cruel martyrdoms of humanity, and so have been able to minister to all its vast and pitiful needs and comfort its voiceless sorrow.

God has no interest in developing a race of mollycoddles. He could work miracles every day, saving children from stubbing their toes and bumping their noses, from tumbling downstairs, from burns when they disobey Mother and touch fire, from being crushed when they run recklessly in front of motor cars, from getting stomachaches when they eat green apples, or from the bitter lot of poverty and neglect when Father ruins himself and his fortune by gambling and drink or when a wicked mother forsakes them and runs off with a new lover. But God does not see fit to work such miracles, and since He does not do it for little children, I see no reason why we should question and vex our hearts and minds because He does not do it for us who are grown up.

Indeed, I think I can see some plausible reasons why He should not do so. We should be more certainly and hopelessly spoiled by such unfailing divine interposition than children spoiled by fond and foolishly indulgent parents. We need discipline, training, forethought, watchfulness, courage, self-restraint, steadfastness, patience, sympathy, faith, forbearance, a proper sense of our own limitations, dependence, and other virtues that unfold our personality and enrich and ennoble character. And God uses these sharp, hard instruments of danger, buffeting, sore and unexpected and inescapable trials and hurts, to develop these virtues in us and, often, through us in others.

He means us no harm. He assures us that "all things work together for good to them that love God" (Rom. 8:28 KJV). Then He leaves us free to believe and prove it and be at peace, or to doubt it, repine, rebel, and suffer needless woes of heart and mind piled on top of every affliction that may overtake us. Let us stir up our faith and sing:

> Since all that I meet shall work for my good,
> The bitter is sweet, the medicine is food.
> Though painful at present, wilt cease before long,
> And then, O! how pleasant, the conqueror's song![5]

When in Honolulu some years ago, I was given a tour of a great sugar mill. There were acres of bewildering machinery working in every direction. There were great iron fingers that grasped the cane, lifting it from the plantation cars and dropping it onto an endless belt that carried it into the merciless grip of great steel rollers that crushed all the sweet juice from the cane and poured its flood into boiling vats. There were fiery furnaces, hissing steam, cogs and wheels and belts, and lifts and plunging chutes defying description, but all working to turn out one hundred pounds of sugar every thirty seconds, so that little boys and girls in New York, London, and country crossroads might have lollipops, soldiers on weary marches might have milk chocolate, sweet June brides might have frosted wedding cakes, kindly old grandmothers might have sugar in their afternoon tea or coffee, and that the whole family might enjoy its Christmas pudding.

So, bewildering as life may seem—with its commingling of joy and sorrow, health and sickness, pleasure and agony, pain and loss, life and death—it is nevertheless all working for the good of those who love God, and preparing us all for the painless, tearless life that shall endless be.

> Behind, a Presence did move
> And grasp me by the hair;
> And a voice in mastery asked, as I strove,
> "Guess now who holds thee." "Death," I said, and there
> The silver answer rang out, "Not Death, but Love."[6]

It is Love who holds us.

NOTES

1. An apparent reference to Robert Browning, "Saul," 1855, public domain. The poem contains the lines, "Each faculty tasked to perceive him, has gained an abyss, where a dewdrop was asked."

2. Edwin O. Excell, "Grace, Enough for Me," 1905, public domain.

3. Rudyard Kipling, "The Enlightenments of Pagett, M. P.," 1919, public domain.

4. George Heath, "My Soul, Be on Thy Guard," 1781, public domain.

5. John Newton, "Begone, Unbelief," 1779, public domain.

6. Edmund Clarence Stedman, ed., *A Victorian Anthology, 1837–1895* (Cambridge: Riverside Press, 1895), accessed September 3, 2015, www.bartleby.com/246/.

Samuel L. Brengle's Holy Life Series

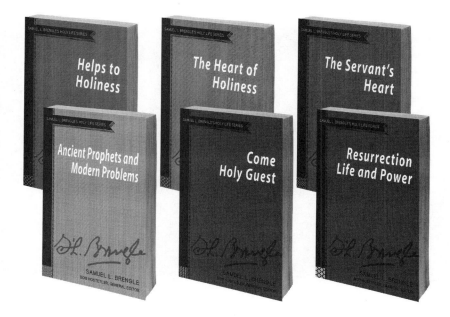

This series comprises the complete works of Samuel L. Brengle, combining all nine of his original books into six volumes, penned by one of the great minds on holiness. Each volume has been lovingly edited for modern readership by popular author (and long-time Brengle devotee) Bob Hostetler. Brengle's authentic voice remains strong, now able to more relevantly engage today's disciples of holiness. These books are must-haves for all who would seriously pursue and understand the depths of holiness in the tradition of John Wesley.

Helps to Holiness
ISBN: 978-1-63257-064-2
eBook: 978-1-63257-065-9

The Heart of Holiness
ISBN: 978-1-63257-066-6
eBook: 978-1-63257-067-3

The Servant's Heart
ISBN: 978-1-63257-068-0
eBook: 978-1-63257-069-7

Ancient Prophets and Modern Problems
ISBN: 978-1-63257-070-3
eBook: 978-1-63257-071-0

Come Holy Guest
ISBN: 978-1-63257-072-7
eBook: 978-1-63257-073-4

Resurrection Life and Power
ISBN: 978-1-63257-074-1
eBook: 978-1-63257-075-8

**Samuel L. Brengle's
Holy Life Series Box Set**
ISBN: 978-1-63257-076-5